DALARA WILLIAMS' theatre credits include, for Belvoir: *Winyanboga Yurringa*; for Ilbijerri Theatre Company: *Black Ties*; for Sydney Theatre Company: *The Visitors*; for Darlinghurst Theatre Company: *Rainbow's End*; for Malthouse Theatre: *Blackie Blackie Brown*; for NIDA; *Realism, Love & Money, The Season at Sarsaparilla, Twelfth Night, The Shadow King, Wulamanayuwi and the Seven Pamanui*.

Film credits include: *The Flood, Top End Wedding*.

Television credits include: *Critical Incident, The Lost Flowers of Alice Hart, Black Comedy S3 & 4, Get Krack!n*.

Short Film credits include: *Last Drinks at Frida's*.

BIG GIRLS DON'T CRY

BY **DALARA WILLIAMS**

CURRENCY PRESS
The performing arts publisher

BELVOIR ST THEATRE

CURRENT THEATRE SERIES

First published in 2025
by Currency Press Pty Ltd,
Gadigal Land, Suite 310, 46–56 Kippax Street, Surry Hills, NSW 2010, Australia
enquiries@currency.com.au
www.currency.com.au

in association with Belvoir

Typeset by Brighton Gray for Currency Press.
Cover image shows Stephanie Somerville, Dalara Williams and Megan Wilding;
photo: Daniel Boud; design by Alphabet Studio.

Currency Press acknowledges the Traditional Owners of the Country on which we
live and work. We pay our respects to all Aboriginal and Torres Strait Islander Elders,
past and present.

Contents

Megan Wilding in rehearsal (Photo: Stephen Wilson Barker)

Guy Simon, Stephanie Somerville, Megan Wilding and Dalara Williams in rehearsal (Photo: Stephen Wilson Barker)

Author's Note

Much of my curiosity for my family history begins within old photo albums. I can't help but start with a very important photograph: from the 1938 Day of Mourning, of a woman holding her child on her hip while her other three children stand up front, the eldest holding a sign that reads, 'Aborigines claim citizenship'. Louisa Ingram (nee) Simpson was her name, my maternal great grandmother. May her bravery and strength continuously show up within the women of her bloodline.

I spent the majority of my life listening to stories of what my family has done as part of the Aboriginal movement of resistance—from the Day of Mourning to the 1965 Freedom Rides, the Foundation of Aboriginal Affairs, Aboriginal Medical Service, Aboriginal Legal Service, the 1972 Tent Embassy and many more actions to defend our sovereignty.

I started my writing journey back in 2017. I was in my third year of NIDA and, for an assessment for my 'Applied Theatre' elective, I interviewed three very important women: my aunty Millie Ingram, Aunty Margret Campbell and my grandmother Norma Ingram. Over a fresh pot of tea, I pressed play on my recording device and asked the women one question: *What was it like to move to Sydney in the sixties?* And the yarns began.

Growing up, I would have heard these stories over various occasions—over dinners, birthdays and reminiscing at the wakes of funerals. These women had told me about the multiple dances they attended at the Foundation of Aboriginal Affairs and other small venues around the city that allowed Aboriginal people in. Stories these women loved to share over and over again and the joy it brought them, reminiscing together, that afternoon. Alongside stories of resistance in a world not built for them, they spoke about the joyous moments of friendship, love and the occasional night of dressing up and dancing. These were stories of like-minded blackfullas coming together and making their time in the big city, doing something blackfullas are good at—making it their own.

After graduating NIDA, I revisited the transcript that had been sitting on my laptop for a year and decided to write something inspired by these women. I started working on *Big Girls Don't Cry*. At first, I wrote it as a screenplay, thinking a film would be a great avenue for this story. That changed in 2023, when I was a part of Ilbijerri's BlackWrights writing program. I made the decision to turn *Big Girls* into a stage play. While I was the 2022 Balnaves Fellow at Belvoir, Dom Mercer thought it would be a great idea to get a couple of actors together and organise a reading of the script. And I thank him for that push. From that, *Big Girls Don't Cry* now premieres as part of Belvoir Street Theatre's 2025 season.

This is a story of everlasting sisterhood, black love and black joy. It's about people wanting to have big dreams and the courage to speak their minds. I wrote this play as a love letter to the women in my life— my grandmothers, mothers, aunties, cousins and sisters—and to the special community of Redfern, Sydney. A community that has birthed so many brilliant minds and sparked so many spirits. I can only hope to uphold the tradition of Redfern, of being unapologetically black.

Thank you to everyone who has championed this story over the years, including my friends who offered their time to sit on my living room floor and read the many versions and drafts of the play. A special thank you to Dom Mercer and Abbie-lee Lewis for helping me navigate these theatre spaces as an emerging writer at Belvoir, and to everyone who has encouraged me to keep going. Thank you to my family for continuously sharing their stories with me over my lifetime, always for a good laugh. My beautiful mother, who has taught me to be the proud and stylish black woman I am today. And to my beautiful friend Megan Wilding—I wrote this play for the two young girls sitting out the back of Eora TAFE, all those years ago, sharing their big dreams and connecting over flowers, rom-coms and The Beatles. Thank you, Megan, for teaching me the meaning of true black sisterhood.

Dalara Williams
February 2025

A love letter to my grandmothers.

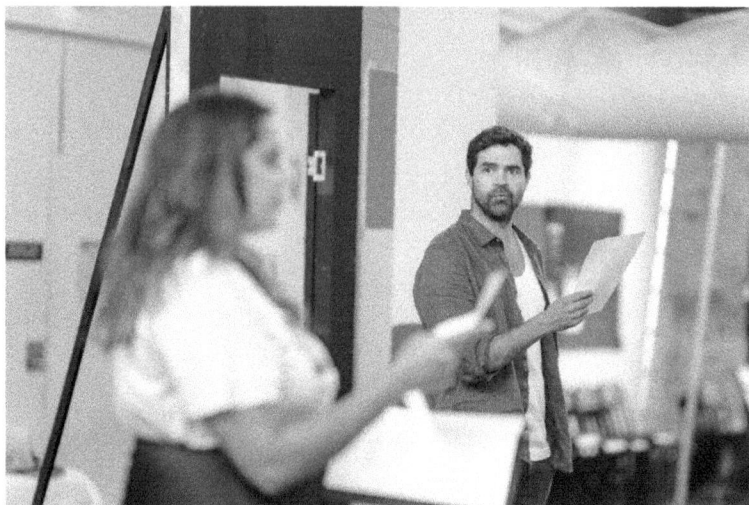

Dalara Williams and Mathew Cooper in rehearsal (Photo: Stephen Wilson Barker)

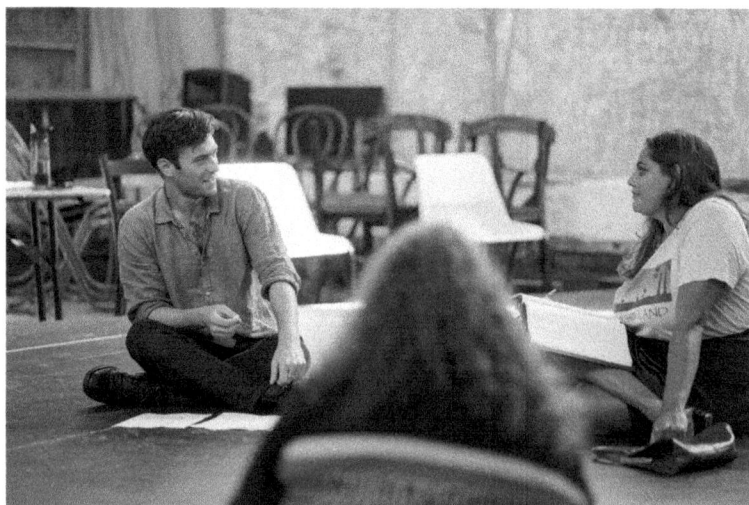

Nic English and Dalara Williams in rehearsal (Photo: Stephen Wilson Barker)

I acknowledge the country this play is based in. Gadigal.
The place of first contact. A place that birthed great loss and sorrow.
It has also reinforced great strength and resistance amongst the first
people. Although the country is covered in concrete and foreign
structure, the land is still here, along with the same waterways
and constellations for thousands of years. That, through our fight
of survival and preservation of ancient practices, we too are still
humans, seeking connections.

Bryn Chapman Parish in rehearsal (Photo: Stephen Wilson Barker)

Megan Wilding, Guy Simon, Stephanie Somerville and Dalara Williams in rehearsal (Photo: Stephen Wilson Barker)

Big Girls Don't Cry was first produced by Belvoir St Theatre, Gadigal Country, Sydney, on 5 April 2025, with the following cast:

OFFICER ROBINSON	Bryn Chapman Parish
MICHAEL	Mathew Cooper
MILO	Nic English
ERNIE	Guy Simon
LULU	Stephanie Somerville
QUEENIE	Megan Wilding
CHERYL	Dalara Williams

Director, Ian Michael
Set Designer, Stephen Curtis
Lighting Designer, Kelsey Lee
Composer and Sound Designer, Brendon Boney
Costume Designer, Emma White
Intimacy Coordinator, Chloë Dallimore
Fight Director, Nigel Poulton
Choreographer, Elle Evangelista
Voice Coach, Laura Farrell
Assistant Director, Abbie-lee Lewis

CHARACTERS

CHERYL. Aboriginal Freshwater woman. Cheryl finds herself between a rock and a hard place as she waits for her boyfriend Michael to return from Vietnam. After a year of not hearing from him and not knowing when she'll see him next, she has to make a decision to continue life without him or still hold on.

QUEENIE. Aboriginal Saltwater woman. Queenie is loud and unapologetic, flirting with everyone on site. She's on a mission to prove that black women can do whatever they want, against what the country is telling them what they can and cannot be.

LULU. Aboriginal Saltwater woman. The best dancer in town. Quiet and observant. Lulu wants to see the bright side of life. To love life. To see beauty within a world even when it constantly shows its ugly head.

ERNIE. Aboriginal Freshwater man and Cheryl's younger brother. One of the first Aboriginal men to attend Sydney University for law. Inspired by the black civil rights movement of the USA, more and more people begin to wake up and stand up with Ernie against a government that is doing more harm than good towards his community. From the Freedom Rides, Ernie continues to advocate for the right of his people.

MILO. Italian Anglo-Australian man from Newtown. Growing up with a mother who was brought over to Australia as a war bride and a father that no longer is a part of his life. Milo tries his best to educate himself about the continuous issues in this country while trying to figure out his own identity in this world. He meets Ernie while being part of the Freedom Rides in February 1965, as part of Student Action for Aborigines.

MICHAEL. Aboriginal Saltwater man. Cheryl's boyfriend. A soldier, Michael has been in active duty in Vietnam. Although he writes letters to Cheryl, they have slowly thinned out over the course of his absence. Will he return, or be lost to the war he shouldn't have been a part of in the first place?

OFFICER ROBINSON. Anglo-Australian.

SETTING

The story takes place in Redfern, Sydney, 1966, as the fight for Aboriginal rights becomes more and more prominent.

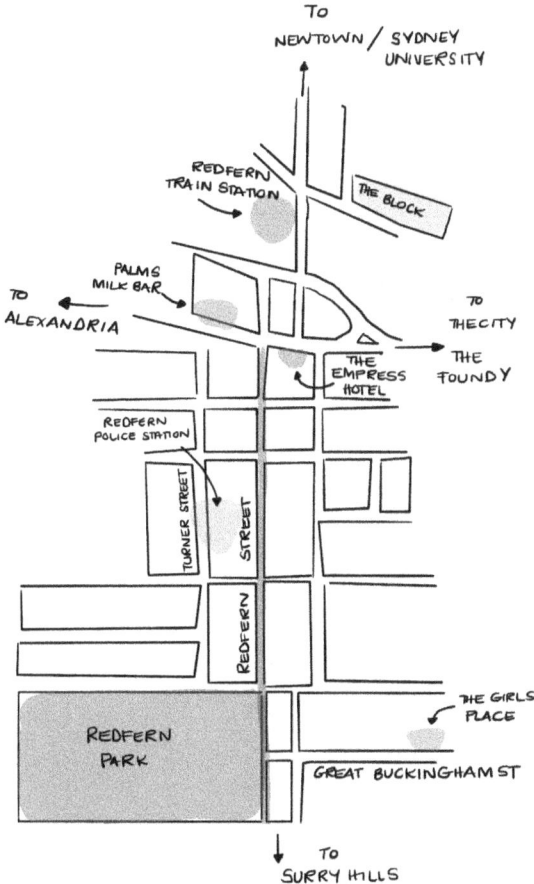

The Foundation for Aboriginal Affairs, 810–812 George Street Sydney: A community organisation for Aboriginal people in Sydney, New South Wales, Australia between 1964 and 1977. Also known as 'The Foundy'.

NOTE

When it comes to characters' age and background, all characters are aged around mid- to late twenties. Even though I know this isn't historically accurate, most of this play is an expression of escapism when it comes to Aboriginal Theatre—that we don't limit our creativity when it comes to these details. As for their background, Redfern is a hub of Aboriginal people from all over the country that migrated to the city for school and/or work. So, the character becomes the actor that portrays them. This story is about dreamers and lovers that find beautiful moments within an uncertain world, and how Aboriginal people continue to find and embody love and joy as part of the resistance.

This playtext went to press before the end of rehearsals and may differ from the play as performed.

SCENE ONE: TWIST AND SHOUT

August.

Great Buckingham Street.

The room is small, a single bed under a wide window facing the street. A worn crochet blanket lays neatly on it. CHERYL *enters, and quickly strips off her work clothes, kicking off her shoes and tossing them near the door.* CHERYL *goes and searches under her bed.*

CHERYL: Queenie?

> *No answer.*

Queenie? Queenie! Where are my shoes?

> *No answer.* CHERYL *spots letters scattered on the bed. She picks them up and starts flicking through them. She goes over and turns on the radio. She sits at her little vanity and begins reading the letters. The sounds of stumbling are heard outside the door.*

LULU: [*offstage*] I hate this city!

> LULU *barges into the room. Flustered.*

Hi. You have hairspray?

CHERYL: Dresser.

> LULU *goes over and grabs the can. She catches her reflection in the mirror.*

LULU: Oh, would you look at this mess.

CHERYL: What happened to you?

LULU: Everything! The people who I'm working for over the bridge.

CHERYL: The white family.

LULU: Yes, the white family. First of all, I spent the whole day cleaning the house. I'm telling you, I did everything. The dishes, the laundry, washed and hung out to dry. I made sure their two children was washed, fed and ready for bed. By the end of the day, spotless. Not a speck of dust. You could run a white glove across the fireplace. But oh no, it wasn't good enough for Mrs Greenhorn. 'Do it again,' she said, 'You missed a spot.' Because she wasn't satisfied with my work, I ended up missing my bus. I had to walk to the train station. In my new shoes mind you, just to find out the train's running late. So, here I am, me on the smallest carriage with these people staring at me for the entire trip. It's not normal.

She takes a last look in the mirror.

That's better. Do you know what happened this time? I found a seat. Not that anyone was willing to give one up for me in the first place. Do you have any blush?

LULU *reaches over and grabs the blush and begins fixing her make up.*

As I sit, I look up and there was this woman. She was wearing this blue fancy coat and pearl necklace. And there she is, this old white woman, clutching her purse, the moment I sat and looked her way. I don't know about you, but these white people always seemed so shocked to see us. The entire trip, from my stop to hers, sitting across from me. Sitting and staring. Looking me up and down with this look of horror. I should have walked right up to her and said 'What are you waiting for, huh? Are you expecting me to pull out a couple of boomerang and start doing corroboree right here in the middle of the carriage for you?' I didn't, but I should have. But how rude was she to stare at me like that?

CHERYL: Or maybe she was looking at you because there's a big tear in your dress.

LULU: What?

LULU *looks down to see the split in her dress.*

Oh no. What am I supposed to do now? I just mended this. You have anything?

CHERYL: Check the bed.

LULU *goes over to the pile of clothes on the bed.*

LULU: What's it like living here?

CHERYL: Why you asking?

LULU: I was thinking, maybe I can move in with you two. Oh, it'll be so much fun, us three living together and save me the trouble with all these horrible busses.

LULU *finds a skirt and begins changing.*

CHERYL: You ever think about going back to country?

LULU: Me? Never.

CHERYL: What about all this nonsense about hating the city?

LULU: I do hate the city, but I won't be able to go out dancing every weekend back home.

CHERYL: You also won't have all this trouble with trains and staring back home either.

LULU: There's nothing back home on country.

CHERYL: You can get a sense of peace there. A nice place to start a family. Ever since Michael left, I don't know what else is keeping me here.

LULU: Trust me, it'll be a lot worse. That's why I should move in with you two. Come on, Sherry. We can work in the factory together. And I'm desperate for work, even if it's a job at the factory. Do you know if they're hiring? I know I don't have much experience, but I'm a fast learner. You know what I'm like, Sherry, you can put in a good word for me. You're great at this kind of stuff. You're pretty and smart and—you're not ready?!

CHERYL: I'm getting there.

LULU *walks over to the radio. She turns it on to a station playing a popular song and begins dancing.*

LULU: You sure? Because the last time we went to a social—

CHERYL: That happened one time, Lulu.

LULU: One time is enough. We missed most of the talent show. I didn't get my chance to show off my new moves I've been practising.

CHERYL: Trust me, Lulu, you'll get your time on the dance floor.

LULU: I better. It's the only time I get to enjoy myself.

LULU *spots the small stack of letters sitting on the bed.*

Are these the letters from Michael?

CHERYL: They sure are.

LULU: Has he sent any photos? He's been away for a while now, I don't think I'd recognise him.

CHERYL *points to a few photos sent through.* LULU *goes over and takes a look.*

Wow, look at him. Not bad at all. I do like a man in uniform, myself.

CHERYL: He does look good.

LULU: You must miss him. I can see he misses you with all of these. What does he say? He must share so many stories about his travels and the types of people he's met.

LULU *pulls out a letter from her purse.*

Oh, this came for you. I wonder if it's from Michael too? What am I saying? Of course it's from him.

CHERYL *goes over and snatches the letters from* LULU *and turns the radio off.*

Hey, don't snatch!

CHERYL: Where did you get this?

LULU: It was on the floor by the door. And why did you have to turn the radio off? I like that song.

CHERYL *looks at the letter.*

Aren't you gonna read it?

CHERYL: I'll read it later.

LULU: Come on. Anything can happen later. You could get hit by a bus or—

CHERYL: Lulu, it's just a letter.

LULU *flicks through the other letters.*

LULU: You ever think about going overseas? You know, leave this place. I don't know what I'll do over there, or the first place I'd go. But it must be something, to see great big buildings, centuries old, or to hear people speak multiple languages and have such different cultures from us. I've been nowhere. I've been to Sydney, home and back again. You know, I've never seen snow before, like real snow from the mountains. But one day I'll get there.

CHERYL *takes the letters and places them in a pile on the dresser.*

QUEENIE: [*offstage*] I told you, Dave, if I catch you again going through my stuff, I'm gonna drag you outside and clock ya in front of everyone!

CHERYL: I got to get a lock for my door.

QUEENIE *barges through the door in a huff, all dressed up and ready to go.*

QUEENIE: I think I'm in love!

CHERYL: With Dave?

QUEENIE: Who? No, not him.

LULU: What happened to Dave?

QUEENIE: I caught the little sneak snooping around my stuff, trying to find things he can hock for money again.

LULU: He's got a big collection of shoes in all sorts of colours too. That's how I got these.

> LULU *takes off her new shoes.*

He did warn me though, said that the shoes were 'hot'. But I told him it didn't bother me if they're hot. Because I'll wear them in the summer and wintertime. You like?

QUEENIE: They're mine.

LULU: How can they be yours? I bought them, so they're mine.

QUEENIE: Give them to me.

> QUEENIE *goes for her shoes, as* LULU *jumps out of the way.* CHERYL *gets up and tries to pull them apart.*

CHERYL: Hold up. Hold on, wait!

> *They stop.*

Queenie, let Lulu borrow the shoes.

QUEENIE/LULU: What?!

CHERYL: Just for tonight.

QUEENIE: Fine, just for tonight. You're lucky I'm in a good mood because I think I've met someone.

LULU: Who?

QUEENIE: The love of my life is who I met.

LULU: Yeah, what's his name?

QUEENIE: He's name? He's name is … Man on bike waiting at the traffic light. He was beautiful. And I'm not gonna say that he looked like Mick Jagger, but he looked like Mick Jagger, you know.

CHERYL: True … for a second, I thought you were gonna say postman.

QUEENIE: Don't you mention postman to me ever again. Ever.

LULU: So what happened to this one?

QUEENIE: Well. He was there on his motorbike. He looked at me and then … he smiled.

LULU: He smiled at you?

QUEENIE: Yes. It was magical.

LULU: Then what happened?

QUEENIE: Nothing. The lights changed, and he rode off into the sunset, never to be seen again. It was like a movie, a real love at first sight.

LULU: Wow.

QUEENIE: I know.

    CHERYL *laughs.*

Why are you laughing?

CHERYL: Nothing.

QUEENIE: What's funny?

LULU: Yeah?

CHERYL: Oh come on, you got to admit it's quite silly for complete strangers to fall in love.

QUEENIE: Why not? White people do it all the time, why not us?

CHERYL: And?

QUEENIE: And, what?

CHERYL: How do you know it's love?

QUEENIE: You just know. It's in their eyes, the way they smile each time they see your face.

LULU: The way they stand next to you, always leaning in wanting to get closer to you.

QUEENIE: You should know this, you've been with Michael for how long?

CHERYL: Yeah, right.

LULU: You felt something like that with Michael, haven't you?

CHERYL: Yes … of course I've felt something like that …

LULU: That's nice.

CHERYL: I need to get ready.

QUEENIE: We got plenty of time.

CHERYL: I promised Ernie I'll be there.

QUEENIE: Let him wait.

CHERYL: Can you get ready?

QUEENIE: I am ready.

CHERYL: Shoes?

LULU: What is the plan, anyways? The Foundy? Clifton?

QUEENIE: Let me guess. We go to The Empress, end up getting arrested and locked up for the night.

LULU: Don't say that, Queenie, it'll be fun. We always have fun at the Big E.

CHERYL *goes over to the bed and pulls out a dress from under the mattress and throws it on.*

CHERYL: Queenie, have you seen the other shoe?

QUEENIE: Maybe Dave hocked it.

LULU: You have anyone to take to the debutante ball yet?

CHERYL: Not yet, but there's plenty of them around.

LULU: It's gonna be a big one too. Mob from all over will be there. We get to dress up in gowns and all the men in tuxedos and learn the waltz. You know, proper partner dancing. The social event of the season.

CHERYL: It doesn't matter really, because Michael is different.

QUEENIE: What is?

CHERYL: This 'love at first sight' nonsense—it was different with Michael.

QUEENIE: Different how?

CHERYL: First, we were friends, and then we got to know each other. From that it eventually turned into something more. Nice. No-one can hold a relationship with electricity alone. You need loyalty, kindness and companionship and when you have that, you both—

QUEENIE: Die from boredom.

LULU: How can you say that, Queenie?

QUEENIE: Um … like this. It sounds boring. For me, not for you, Sherry. For you, it sounds great. Sounds like you're having the time of your life and I'm happy for you, truly I am. But who wants a love like that? Give me fire, give me passion, love and devotion. I want it from the very beginning. As soon as our eyes meet from across the room. And when we do, we'll be like magnets, drawn to each other without knowing why. The electricity shooting between us, going back and forth and back and forth. Eye contact, gentle touches, the intensity.

QUEENIE *sighs.* CHERYL *grabs the other shoe.*

CHERYL: Found it.

LULU: And you had that with someone before?

QUEENIE: Once.

> CHERYL *checks her watch.*

CHERYL: Shit, I'm late.

QUEENIE: We've got plenty of time.

LULU: Actually, we don't.

QUEENIE: By the sound of things, you clearly need excitement in your life, Sherry. Aren't you sick of going to work all day and sitting at home all night?

CHERYL: I'm going out tonight.

QUEENIE: Yeah, to see your brother.

CHERYL: Well, it's been forever since I've seen him, and he said he had something to show me.

> CHERYL *continues to get ready quickly.*

QUEENIE: What's with her?

LULU: Sherry got a letter from Michael.

QUEENIE: Oh she did, did she? And here I thought you would be excited to hear from your love. What does he write to you, anyways?

> QUEENIE *reaches for the pile.*

Here, let me read them.

CHERYL: Don't you dare!

LULU: Read it, read it.

CHERYL: No!

LULU: Come on, Sherry, you're so lucky.

CHERYL: Can we leave it?

QUEENIE: Yeah, you get to come home to a mailbox full of love letters in messy handwriting, telling you how much he's missed you and he's been thinking of you. That he can't wait to come back home to see you, so he can marry you, have babies with you and live happily ever after.

LULU: A soldier off at war and his sweetheart waiting at home for him to return. Lost and alone in a foreign country. He writes to her every day to remind her of his love and even though he's on the other side of the world fighting a war, he's doing it for her.

QUEENIE: See, Lulu gets it.

CHERYL: I thought you didn't want an easy love.

QUEENIE: I don't, but you do.

> CHERYL *quickly stashes the letters away in a shoebox.*

What do you think, should I go with this dress?

CHERYL: What do you mean, I need 'easy love'?

QUEENIE: Nothing. It means you like it easy. You're with Michael anyways, so why does it matter? So, the dress, what do we think about the dress?

CHERYL: If you're not happy, you got plenty of other dresses to try on.

QUEENIE: Maybe I will try on other dresses.

CHERYL: Maybe you should.

QUEENIE: I will! And it'll be the best dress ever and everyone will be jealous of me, including you.

LULU: What's wrong with the dress?

QUEENIE: It's … nice, it's sweet. But I need something bold and bright and out there, something that tells the world that I've arrived. You know what I mean?

LULU: Who you looking pretty for?

QUEENIE: Myself. I look good because I want to look good. Those around me better step up or move along.

> QUEENIE *goes and puts her shoes on and looks at her dress one more time.*

You're right, Sherry. This is the dress. I'm gonna make so many people jealous. It's just missing something.

CHERYL: No pearls. Queenie, can't I have one thing you don't get your grubby little hands on?

QUEENIE: My hands aren't grubby. When are they grubby?

LULU: They're not grubby.

QUEENIE: You sure?

LULU: They're not grubby.

QUEENIE: Okay. But I look good, right?

LULU: You're fine.

QUEENIE: Fine isn't good. I'm not dressed like this for 'fine'. Great, maybe. Beautiful. A goddess even, but 'fine'?

LULU: Queenie, walk out the door.

QUEENIE: So, what am I, fine or good?!

LULU: You're fine!

> QUEENIE *and* LULU *exit.* CHERYL *stops at the door. She walks over to the bed and picks up the shoebox and opens it.*

[*Offstage*] Sherry!

> *She takes a letter and stashes it in her purse. She exits.*

SCENE TWO: OOO BABY BABY

Redfern Street.

CHERYL *stands in the street and pulls out a letter from her purse. She opens and reads.* MICHAEL *enters wearing an army uniform with a newspaper in hand. He reads.*

MICHAEL: March twelfth, 1965. My dearest Cheryl-Lee. You know, I thought of you the other day. I was walking through the base. You see the usual things around you, tents here and there, and trees all throughout. Some days I try to imagine the tall gum trees from back home. The smell of eucalypts as the rain hits the leaves for the first time. Anyways, there's this one tree in base. Has signs, plaques with different cities pointing in each direction. You have Hong Kong, Singapore, Auckland. And one that says 'Sydney', pointing right at you. I saw that sign, which of course made me think of you. It made me think about how we first met. You remember? At the Foundation, right? It was … what night was it? I think it was a Saturday. You were wearing this yellow dress, that kind of made your skin glow and shine under the lights. And those legs …

It's a shame I can't be there with you. To see you in that dress again. But I try to keep up as best I can with everything happening back home. Ernie sent me a clipping of paper from back there.

> *He reads the article.*

'All over Australia, tribute is now being paid to a courageous group of Sydney University students who have become known as the "Freedom Riders". They could not be moved from their determination. A most important tribute to their work has been the way they have won the confidence of many Aboriginal people, as seen by the way Aboriginal children at Moree demonstrated for entry into the baths after the students left the town.' As soon as someone has a paper from back home, I'm usually one of the first to jump on it.

I've met a few people. Trust me, it's not all doom and gloom in Nui Dat. We're about over two hours from Saigon, the city. Let me tell you, I never been to a place like this. People everywhere, traffic, cars zooming left and right. I've even been to some of the local bars here. A couple of them. And they let me in, no questions asked. I walk right in, get a little one of these.

He nods his head in greeting.

A boy can get use to this. They treat me like everyone else, especially if I wear the uniform—I'll send a photo. You have to tell me what you think. Does it suit me? I look good, aye?

CHERYL *furrows her brow.*

You need to stop that. Stop worrying, especially about me. You know, leaving you had to be one of the hardest and dumbest decisions I made in my life. But I know it'll be worth it. It's just something we have to do. Like my father and grandfather did before me. A rite of passage, I guess—we have to do things even if we don't like it. Even if it kills us. Everything will be fine. I'm safe, I promise. This won't be forever. Okay? Michael.

SCENE THREE: GIMMIE SOME LOVIN'

Regent Street.

The Empress Hotel.

One of the few pubs that allows Aboriginal patrons. It's busy and loud.

QUEENIE: So here we are. Again.

LULU: Don't be like that, Queenie, it's going to be fun. Look, there's Ernie.

QUEENIE: Yeah, is there anyone else we can talk to?

LULU: Come on.

CHERYL *crosses the room, bumping into* MILO *and almost spilling his drink.*

MILO: Whoa.

CHERYL: Oh, I'm sorry. I didn't—
MILO: It's okay.
CHERYL: I didn't get any on—
MILO: Yeah, no, I don't think you got me. No. I think we're clear.
CHERYL: Good.

> CHERYL *turns.*

MILO: Leaving so soon?
CHERYL: Sorry?
MILO: You almost knocked my drink, let me buy you a new one.
CHERYL: I don't think it works like that.
MILO: It could if you let it.

> QUEENIE *calls out to* CHERYL.

CHERYL: Sorry for the … thing … the drink. I really didn't mean to …
MILO: It was nothing.

> *Beat.*

Don't let me hold you up.

> CHERYL *catches up with them.*

QUEENIE: Sherry can decide. Foundy or Shrublands?
LULU: I suggested Shrublands.
QUEENIE: I just don't want to walk, Lulu, you know how I feel about that.
LULU: Why did you ask then?

> ERNIE, CHERYL*'s brother, interrupts with a drink in hand.*

ERNIE: Hey, what took you so long?
LULU: We got caught up.
QUEENIE: Sherry was late.
LULU: We had to stop every two seconds because Queenie wanted to talk to everyone who looked her way.
QUEENIE: Don't blame me, it's not my fault everyone wants to talk to me. I can't help it, it comes natural. People gravitate towards me.
ERNIE: Yeah, that's the reason.
QUEENIE: What?
ERNIE: That's your thing, right? You'll go anywhere where someone would give you the tiniest bit of attention.

QUEENIE: Don't start me, Ernest.

ERNIE: You just said you give every Tom, Dick and Harry the time of day—why not me?

QUEENIE: Because it's you. Look, Ernest, I'm allowed to be nice to people. I can talk to every person in this building if I want.

ERNIE: Yeah, you're really doing the people a service.

QUEENIE: That's rich coming from you.

ERNIE: What is that supposed to mean?

QUEENIE: I know what you think of us. Now that you go to that little university of yours—

ERNIE: Little university.

QUEENIE: Yes, little university. You look down upon us common folks as if we know nothing about the real world.

ERNIE: Because you know nothing about the real world, Queenie.

QUEENIE: Is that right?

ERNIE: You know I'm right.

QUEENIE: You're lucky we're in a public place or I'll—

ERNIE: Or you'll do what, Queenie?

> QUEENIE *tries her best to hold her tongue.*

QUEENIE: You know what, you're not worth my time. I'm not going to stand here and put up with this. I'm gonna get myself a drink and maybe talk to a few people. You coming, Lulu?!

> QUEENIE *exits.*

LULU: We're gonna get some drinks.

> *She exits.* CHERYL *hits* ERNIE.

ERNIE: What was that for?

CHERYL: You know, you really need to ease up on Queenie.

ERNIE: Come on, she knows I'm mucking around.

CHERYL: Does she though?

ERNIE: Queenie's just being Queenie, she sits there and expect everyone to jump.

CHERYL: It doesn't help when you're always finding something to dig.

ERNIE: It's fun.

> ERNIE *takes a sip from his drink.*

CHERYL: I got a letter from Mum today.

ERNIE: Disappointed?

CHERYL: It would be good if you wrote home once in a while. You need to pull your finger out. Where have you been, anyways? It seems like forever since I've seen you myself—

ERNIE: Don't start doing this again, Sherry.

CHERYL: What's wrong with me wanting to spend time with my little brother?

ERNIE: That's the thing, I'm not little anymore. I'm old. I'm a man now.

CHERYL: A man.

ERNIE: Yes, a man. Things are different. I've got stuff going on.

CHERYL: Really, like what?

ERNIE: The world. It's all changing and one way or another I'm gonna be part of that change.

CHERYL: Gorn, don't get a big head now.

ERNIE: I'm not.

CHERYL: 'I'm gonna be a part of that change, I'm gonna rally these people and rise up from the ashes.'

ERNIE: Joke all you want sis. This is Redfern. Anything can happen for us here and whatever happens, I am gonna be that change. Take a look at this.

ERNIE *hold up a newspaper.*

CHERYL: Oh come on, Ernie, why now?

ERNIE: Just listen, will ya? 'Land Rights for Aboriginal People.' Two hundred Aboriginal workers and their families walk-off as protest at Wave Hill Cattle Station in the Northern Territory.

CHERYL: Two hundred people?

ERNIE: This is the revolution. What we've been working for. We had the Freedom Rides. Everything that's going on with the Foundation. This referendum coming up. Now this walk-off. What's next? This country has done everything to get rid of us. Not just 'then'—oh, they love reminding us that. Always saying, 'back then, back then'. But it wasn't just 'back then'; it's now and every time in between since they planted that godforsaken flag in our land. Years of lies upon lies, forcing their superiority on us. Telling us where we can walk, what place we can go or not go. For us to stay right where we are and take it, as if this life is our destiny, a fate we must accept.

You think I was born into this world to have these white people treat me like a farm animal? Is that what they think? That this is all part of natural selection? Nah, fuck that. But you know what? Let them stand there in their entitlement. Let them think, let them believe that they're smarter than us. They can twist and turn their truth all they want to make them sleep better at night, but right now? People are waking up. People are seeing the truth. And I'm not slowing down for no-one. You've seen it—when people come together and stand for what they believe in. You've been there, Sherry, you've felt it. The power that we create when we come together. It's like that buzz in the air, right before a thunderstorm hits. We're that storm, Sherry.

MILO *enters, catching the end of* ERNIE*'s speech.*

CHERYL: You sound like one of those hippies.

ERNIE: You better get with the times or get left behind.

MILO: Don't you get sick of the sound of your own voice?

ERNIE: Aye, look who fucking made it. How long has it been?

MILO: Too long.

ERNIE: That mine?

MILO *hands him a drink.*

MILO: You don't stop, do you?

ERNIE: Welcome to the one and only 'Empress Hotel'. This right here is the world my friend, our world and we don't have the luxury to stop. Not everyone can opt out of this skin we're in. Trust me, I've tried.

MILO: Is that so?

ERNIE: Because, unlike you, this system here wasn't built for people like us.

MILO: And you think it was built for a wog like me?

ERNIE: Most of it. You'll be an outsider until they need numbers and just like that, you'll be one of them, no sign of your wog heritage except the name you carry. Shouldn't you be over there in 'Nam fighting with the rest of them?

MILO: I should be asking you the same question, you know, fighting for your country and all.

ERNIE: What country? I look around to see the same faces as mine, continuously getting the short end of this shit stick.

MILO: Okay, you've won. Your life is more of a shit show than mine.

ERNIE: You're learning.

    CHERYL *clears her throat.*

Here, I want you to meet someone. This is my sister, Sherry. This is Milo. We met on the Freedom Rides.

CHERYL: Freedom Rides. That must have been quiet an experience.

ERNIE: When I first met him, as soon as we got into Walgett, this one here almost got his arse bitten by a brown snake.

MILO: Sorry? If my memory serves me correctly, it was *you.*

ERNIE: Lies. It wasn't me. I know I can handle a brown snake.

MILO: I think you've been living in the city a little too long to handle anything out there in the bush.

ERNIE: Shut the fuck up!

    Someone calls out to ERNIE *from across the bar.*

Huh? One sec. I'll be right back. Talk, talk. / Yeah, what do you want?!

CHERYL: Ah, Ernie—

    MILO *and* CHERYL *smile to each other.*

MILO: Hi.

CHERYL: Hi.

MILO: You're Ernie's sister?

CHERYL: The last time I checked I was.

MILO: Sherry?

CHERYL: Yes.

MILO: Milo.

CHERYL: I heard / Ernie mention it.

MILO: Right, right. From before. When Ernie said he had a sister I thought you would be—Not that you look like Ernie in any way / —I mean that—

CHERYL: I don't?

MILO: No, I meant you look like you can be related in some way. I didn't mean that you look like him in …

CHERYL: You seem nervous.

MILO: Me? No, I don't think so …

CHERYL: It's okay, most people are when they first come around here. It's not everyone's cup of tea.

MILO: Does it look like it's my first time here?

CHERYL *has a good look at him.*

'Cause I'm white?

CHERYL: Didn't you say you were?

MILO: You're right, I'm not but I'm also not …

CHERYL: Where do you live?

MILO: Newtown.

CHERYL: Ah.

MILO: Is there something wrong with Newtown?

CHERYL: I didn't say anything was wrong.

MILO: But you did. You made a sound.

CHERYL: Right.

MILO: Yeah, you went, 'Ah.'

CHERYL: Ah. And that means what exactly?

MILO: That you have an issue with me being from Newtown.

CHERYL: You said it, not me.

MILO *takes a sip from his drink.*

MILO: Can I buy you a drink?

CHERYL: I have someone getting me one. I see you still have yours.

MILO: Yeah. Almost lost it a moment ago. It gets busy in here, hey. I had someone completely push right into me earlier.

CHERYL: Yeah, it gets like that in here.

MILO: My drink was this close to going everywhere. It didn't, but if it did, it would have been a shame to ruin the pretty dress they were wearing.

CHERYL: Well, whoever knocked your drink owes you a new one.

MILO: I can't do that.

CHERYL: It's the rules, isn't it? The unspoken etiquette of buying a round of drinks at your local public house.

MILO: Like offering to buy the prettiest girl here a drink. That kind of rules?

ERNIE *returns.*

ERNIE: How's it going here?

CHERYL: Good.

MILO: Good.

CHERYL: Milo was just telling me that he lives in Newtown.

ERNIE: First time here, aye?

CHERYL: You don't cross the tracks that often?

MILO: Had no reason to, but I think that'll change tonight.

ERNIE: Well, you're welcomed to the Big E anytime.

LULU *and* QUEENIE *enter with drinks.*

LULU: You know the rules!

QUEENIE: [*sarcastically*] Oh that's right, because you think I can't handle myself? This poor little black girl can't do anything. Another white man comes over and tries to infiltrate me and break my women's circle. What?! I can't talk to a few fellas? They could have been a couple of allies.

ERNIE: When have you ever used the term 'allies'?

QUEENIE: You're not the only learned one here.

LULU: I'm not allowing these white men to take up anymore of our time.

QUEENIE: First of all, his name is Brian. We used to live next door to each other when I first moved down here. Lovely fella.

LULU: I'm talking about the men at the bar.

QUEENIE: Oh. Them.

QUEENIE *gives them a little wave from across the bar.*

ERNIE: What, you too good to socialise with us?

QUEENIE: I see you all the time.

ERNIE: When?

LULU: I saw them before we even got to the bar. Quickly made a beeline straight for her.

ERNIE: Typical.

QUEENIE: Hey!

ERNIE: It's true.

QUEENIE: What, Ernest, upset I wasn't talking to you?

ERNIE: You're hilarious.

CHERYL: Will you two give it a rest?

LULU: So, I tap one of them on the shoulder and said, 'Hi, can we help you? Because if you'd like to sit with us, you need to go ahead and shout the table.' There, clear as day. But they stood there looking at me as if I spoke French. So, I repeated, 'shout the table or leave', and what did they do?

ERNIE: Leave.

LULU: The type of men you attract, Queenie, is beyond me.

QUEENIE: I'm a good listener.

LULU: Please. They just want someone they can tell their pity story to for free and somehow, it's always you. What was the story tonight? He had to give up his football career because he had a child on the way.

ERNIE: That's exactly how they get you, Queenie. One minute you're free, doing your own thing. Then these strangers come over, lost. Helpless in this new place. So, you start feeling bad, decide to help them out, just this once out the goodness of your heart, and then bam!

> ERNIE *hits the table and waves his hand over to* QUEENIE*'s direction like he's performing a magic trick.*

Assimilated.

QUEENIE: Where's my lemon squash?

LULU: Why?

QUEENIE: You want this drink in your face?

ERNIE: Bring it.

> QUEENIE *grabs her drink.*

CHERYL: Queenie, don't do this, you're letting him get to you again.

QUEENIE: Nah, I've had enough of this.

> QUEENIE *stops, apotting* MILO *standing with the group.*

Hi …

> QUEENIE *tries to compose herself. Taking a sip from her drink and looking at* MILO.

Who's this? He's cute.

MILO: Thanks.

ERNIE: [*to* MILO] Don't pay her no mind.

QUEENIE: Excuse me? Don't be rude, Ernest, introduce me to your friend.

ERNIE: Why?

> QUEENIE *shoots* ERNIE *daggers before smiling and offering* MILO *her hand.*

QUEENIE: Queenie.

MILO: Emilio.

QUEENIE: Oh, Emilio. Where's that from?

MILO: It's Italian. My mother is—

QUEENIE: That's so beautiful. I love it. Emilio. Emiiillioo. Doesn't it just roll off your tongue. Emilio. Where did you find this one, Ernest?

MILO: School.

QUEENIE: Oh, you go to university with Ernest? You must be … smart.

MILO: I can be.

ERNIE: We met during the Freedom Rides.

QUEENIE: That bus thing? That happened a year ago, and we're just meeting you now. Why have you been hiding him, Ernest?

MILO: I—

ERNIE: Wanted to save him the embarrassment of meeting you. Now, you done?

QUEENIE: Oh, I'm just getting started. Emilio, would you like a drink?

ERNIE: You don't have to.

QUEENIE: Don't listen to him, he doesn't know what he's talking about.

> MILO *follows* QUEENIE *towards the bar.*

LULU: I wonder what 'man on bike' thinks.

ERNIE: Who?

LULU: Queenie's crushes that come and go as fast as day turns to night.

ERNIE: She does that a lot, doesn't she?

CHERYL: What did you say before? Queenie is just being Queenie.

> OFFICER ROBINSON *appears. He wanders through the pub.*

ERNIE: Curfew starting early tonight? Pub doesn't close for hours.

ROBINSON: Just checking up on things. See that there's no trouble going on here.

ERNIE: No trouble here. Just people trying to enjoy themselves. You don't have to be here.

ROBINSON: How much have you been drinking, sir?

ERNIE: 'Sir'? You know that's the first time one of you have called me that. I never thought you had it your vocabulary.

ROBINSON: I'm gonna have to ask you all to leave.

ERNIE: On what premise?

ROBINSON: This is my district and I'll make sure to protect the people of it.

ERNIE: And we're not the people? The owner said we're allowed to be here.

ROBINSON: There's been some complaints.

ERNIE: Complaints now?

ROBINSON: Noise complaints. That people are making a ruckus along those side paths.

ERNIE: Maybe you should be out there, looking for them.

ROBINSON: Are you calling me a liar?

ERNIE: You guys don't really have the reputation of being honest.

ROBINSON: You getting smart with me, boy?

ERNIE: Just helping you do your job.

> OFFICER ROBINSON *steps closer to* ERNIE. *He doesn't move, holding his ground, not breaking eye contact.*

ROBINSON: Move it along and don't make me say it again.

> OFFICER ROBINSON *turns around.*

ERNIE: This is complete bullshit and you know it.

> OFFICER ROBINSON *stops and reaches for his baton.*

ROBINSON: What did you say, boy?

ERNIE: I said this is—

CHERYL: Nothing, officer, he said nothing.

ERNIE: No, he heard me.

CHERYL: We're moving along, sir. I'm waiting on a friend, I don't want her walking home alone so late at night. We're leaving.

ROBINSON: Good! We have enough trouble with you lot as it is. [*To* ERNIE] And *you.* You better watch that mouth of yours, boy.

> OFFICER ROBINSON *leaves.* ERNIE *starts following him but is stopped by* CHERYL.

CHERYL: Are you serious, Ernie?!

> ERNIE *skulls his drink.*

Why do you always do that?

ERNIE: Do what?

CHERYL: You open your mouth and stuff like—

ERNIE: I told you, I'm not staying silent anymore. You can walk though this world blindfolded all you want. He knew exactly what he was doing. *Boy.* That's what he said. And what did you do?

CHERYL: Sorry I stopped you from spending a night at the station—

ERNIE: Oh, come on, you know exactly what they're doing.

CHERYL: Aren't you tired of this?

ERNIE: Aren't you?! Don't you see? This is what I've been trying to tell you. Thinking they can keep their boot on our necks and we'll be happy and smile and give them a pat on the back for allowing us to live here along with them—here, on the land that was rightfully ours in the first place. It's a fucking game to them. They dance on that line to see how far they can cross it. Guys like that get a kick out of pushing people like us around.

CHERYL: Why give them the satisfaction? Why give them another reason to throw you in the back of the paddy wagon and lock you —

ERNIE: I didn't do anything, we didn't do anything! I'm not gonna stand around and let these white cunts walk all over us anymore.

> ERNIE *storms off.*

SCENE FOUR: WALKING AFTER MIDNIGHT

Regent Street.

Empress Hotel.

Everyone exits, leaving CHERYL *alone. She takes in the night air, inhaling deep, trying to calm herself down. She reaches into her purse and pulls out a letter from* MICHAEL. *She looks at it.* MILO *enters.*

MILO: Come out for some fresh air?

> CHERYL *looks over to see* MILO. MILO *pulls out a cigarette and lights it. He offers one to* CHERYL. *She shakes her head no. He nods as he takes a draw.*

Nice night tonight.

> CHERYL *looks up to the sky. They both stand there in silence.* MILO *takes another draw.*

You have a good night.

> *He begins to head back inside.*

CHERYL: You're a student, aye?

> MILO *stops.*

With Ernie. That's how you met with the whole umm … 'Students … students … '

MILO: 'Student Action for Aborigines.'

CHERYL: That's right. 'Student Action for Aborigines.' You liked it, doing stuff like that?

MILO: Don't think we're meant to, but it's something I wanted to do.

CHERYL: Why?

MILO: I'm sure you've heard plenty of stories from Ernie.

CHERYL: He has. But I'm asking you.

MILO: It was … eye opening.

CHERYL: You survived though. Those towns, I mean. It's good, not a lot of people do.

MILO: Right. Yeah, I guess we survived.

> *Beat.*

I should get back inside.

CHERYL: Yeah. Yes. You better be careful in there; The Empress isn't the best place to start trouble. You don't want to ruin your night.

MILO: The night's still young. I'm sure there's plenty of opportunities for it to get ruined. It was lovely to meet you, Cheryl.

> MILO *exits.* CHERYL *looks at her letter and tries to smooth the creases before putting it back into her purse.* LULU *and* QUEENIE *enter.*

QUEENIE: Argh, my feet are killing me! I wouldn't be in so much pain if Ernest would stop stepping on my foot.

LULU: Hey, maybe you should ask Ernie to be your partner for the deb?

QUEENIE: You got to be joking. Ernest is the last person I want to dance with. He's like a giant toddler unable to control his limbs.

LULU: What is it with you two? Always fighting.

QUEENIE: Me fighting with—he's always fighting with me.

LULU: Right.

QUEENIE: No, I'm going to make my debut alone, where I'll be crowned Miss Waratah.

LULU: You, Miss Waratah?

QUEENIE: Yes.

LULU: I mean, you think you can become Miss Waratah?

QUEENIE: Why are you saying it like that? I don't know why it's hard for you people to believe in me. To believe that maybe I can be crowned. I could be a great Miss Waratah! And when I am announced, I'll sit on that float covered in flowers, travelling through the city where everyone is there to see *me*. And I'll stand and wave as they throw rose petals to celebrate me. It'll be perfect, like my hair.

> QUEENIE *notices* CHERYL *standing there, quiet.*

What's wrong with you?

CHERYL: Nothing.

QUEENIE: We're not gonna talk about what happened back there? With Ernest?

CHERYL: I don't think there's much to talk about.

LULU: We know what he's like.

QUEENIE: I do. You got to admit he's good at what he does.

LULU: I'm surprised you notice, Queenie, since you were too busy making doe eyes at Ernie's new friend.

QUEENIE: There's nothing wrong with me being kind.

CHERYL: You?

QUEENIE: I am kind! Besides, it's nice to have someone around since Michael is away.

LULU: You say it as if he's away on some sort of holiday.

QUEENIE: I didn't mean it like that.

CHERYL: We all have our part in this. Joining the army was Michael's way of doing his.

LULU: You can only hope things will get better, so he can finally come back.

QUEENIE: Things aren't getting better though.

LULU: I thought things were finally changing.

QUEENIE: Lulabelle, you must be spending too much time over that bridge with the white folks for your too-little sixpence, to think things are changing here. Of course we want to have a better life. That's why we moved to the city in the first place. Our new home away from home, to seek more than what they've been telling us. We may have moved off the missions to find it but as always, the mission manager mentality seems to follow us wherever we go. I want to be able to dream, just like the next person. But this country—right now—they don't want to see us as anything more than just blacks.

Beat.

What are you doing, you staying at ours tonight?

LULU: Looks like it, there's no way I'm getting over the bridge tonight. We walking?

QUEENIE: Ugh, walking!

LULU: We always have a great time walking.

QUEENIE: Not when my feet are bleeding.

LULU: Then get better shoes. Come on, Queenie.

LULU *sings the first verse of 'Walkin' After Midnight' by Patsy Cline.*

QUEENIE: No, I'm not doing this.

CHERYL: Just take your shoes off.

QUEENIE: I'm not putting my feet on this dirty ground. I'll ask a ride from a police officer before I walk through these streets barefooted.

CHERYL *joins in dancing with* LULU.

LULU *continues singing 'Walkin' After Midnight'.*

CHERYL: Hurry up, Queenie!

QUEENIE: Agh, fine. Wait up!

QUEENIE *removes her shoes and runs off after the girls, as they continue to sing.*

SCENE FIVE: YOU REALLY GOT A HOLD ON ME

Regent Street.

Palms Milk Bar. ERNIE *and* MILO *enter and pull up a seat at the closest table.*

MILO: You made that up.

ERNIE: I don't make the rules. I break them.

MILO: Your mother would be proud.

ERNIE: She taught me how. That woman used to plant herself in front of the police station when things weren't great on the mission. She did it so much the police knew her by name.

MILO: Apple doesn't fall far from the tree.

ERNIE: So, you're gonna hear it again until it's imprinted on your brain.

MILO: Go ahead.

ERNIE: You listening?

MILO: I'm listening.

ERNIE: 'Section Twenty-One: The Parliament shall, subject to this Constitution, have power to make laws for the peace, order and good government of the Commonwealth with respect to: The people of any race, other than the aboriginal people in any state, for whom it is necessary to make special laws.' And—

> ERNIE *is about to speak but is cut off by* MILO.

MILO: Section One Hundred and Twenty-Seven: 'In reckoning the numbers of people of the Commonwealth, or of a State or other part of the Commonwealth, aboriginal natives should not be counted.'

> *Beat.*

After hours of being cramped on the bus with you, I think I have the entire constitution memorised.

ERNIE: Too bad you're not as good at chess as you think you are.

MILO: And somehow chess is related to what is happening to us today?

ERNIE: Of course it is. You can easily be a little pawn whose duty is to protect the crown. To serve people that are new to this land. And us, we're just forgotten. A bunch of savages, nomads, wandering this great land and not knowing what to do with it. And now it's run into the ground by a bunch of people here idolising a monarch and country like the United Kingdom when most of them—not all of them—most of them are here in this little place we call 'Australia' because the country they hold such loyalty to kicked their ancestors out.

> ERNIE *laughs.*

It's ridiculous, right? Don't they stop for a just a second and listen to themselves speak? Do they hear the things they say? Nah, the only way we're getting through this is if we play the game the same way as these old white men in power and outwit them.

MILO: Play them at their own game, you say.

ERNIE: Take Vietnam. I don't know how some of these fellas make the decision to leave. Family, honour to serve, something to do. I could never do what he's doing. Even the thought of leaving this country with a chance of no return—it's a big fucking decision. Couldn't be me, I got too much to do here.

MILO: Sherry said the same thing.

ERNIE: When?

MILO: In passing.

ERNIE: In passing where?

MILO: What's with the third degree?

ERNIE: Hey, I'm wondering.

MILO: Okay.

ERNIE: You sweet on her or something?

MILO: What? No, I'm not—no.

ERNIE: [*teasing*] I don't know. It sounds like you have a thing for my sister. Which I might warn you is a big mistake, if you ask me.

MILO: Lucky I'm not. I could say the same thing with you and Queenie.

ERNIE: With me and Queenie? Please.

MILO: What's this back-and-forth you two got going on?

ERNIE: Nothing is going on. She's someone that gets on my nerves, that's all.

MILO: Sure she is.

> CHERYL *enters. She looks around for any sign of the girls and realises she must be the first there.*

CHERYL: Ernie, Milo, hi. I'm surprised to see you on these sides of the tracks.

MILO: I have my reasons.

ERNIE: Well, I love to stay, but I have to get going.

CHERYL: Aren't you gonna stay? Queenie and Lulu will be here any minute.

ERNIE: Can't. I got this thing.

MILO: What thing?

ERNIE: You know.

MILO: No, I don't.

ERNIE: Yeah, remember? The thing, I can't miss out on it. Sorry I can't stay, sis. Love ya.

CHERYL: Okay.

> ERNIE *kisses* CHERYL *on the cheek and leaves.*

What thing?

MILO: Beats me.

> *They don't move.*

You want to sit?

CHERYL: I don't want to intrude.

MILO: Please.

CHERYL: Really, I can find another / place to—

MILO: I'm really good company. Promise.

> CHERYL *goes and sits.*

So.

> MILO *notices the letter in hand.*

That's a pretty worn letter you got there. Michael's?

CHERYL: Yeah.

MILO: How did you both meet?

CHERYL: You don't want to know.

> MILO *waits.*

Okay … um … we met at the Foundation. I don't know if you know anything about the …

MILO: Ernie keeps me informed.

CHERYL: Right. Well … I was there with Queenie and Lulu. One night, I went into the back room, towards the kitchen to make myself a cup of tea, and there he was, standing around the pool table with a few of the other fellas. He was wearing this crisp white shirt and tie. Very handsome. He always made sure he looked presentable wherever he went. I made my tea and tried to quietly snake my way past the table, not wanting to get roped into one of Ernie's rants. The next thing I know, I turn right into Michael, spilling my tea all over his white shirt. Poor guy had to spend the rest of the evening with a tea-stained shirt.

> CHERYL *laughs to herself.*

He didn't tell me for the longest time that he was planning to leave.

> *Pause.*

You know anyone over … That went over?

MILO: I knew a few.

CHERYL: And did any of them come back?

> MILO *doesn't answer.*

Are you always like this?

MILO: What do you mean?

CHERYL: Look around. How many white boys are sitting here listening to one of us?

MILO: The difference is, I'm not a white boy.

> LULU *and* QUEENIE *enter.*

LULU: Oh my goodness, I completely forgot Johnny worked here.

QUEENIE: Johnny? Who's Johnny?

LULU: You know, Johnny Townsend.

CHERYL: You're late.

QUEENIE: You're early.

LULU: I told you about him, you know, tall, skinny, kind of shy. We got to talking the other day, when he was closing up.

QUEENIE: Oh right, Johnny, who works here.

LULU: I asked him to be my partner for the debutante, remember?

QUEENIE: Already.

LULU: Not yet, but I'm gonna. Look there he is now. I'll go over and say a quick hello. Wish me luck.

> LULU *leaves.*

QUEENIE: That girl is going to make a complete fool of herself.

MILO: And none of you are going to stop her.

QUEENIE/CHERYL: No.

QUEENIE: Well hello, Mr Emilio, la vita è bella.

MILO: La vita è bella.

CHERYL: And all of a sudden you speak Italian?

QUEENIE: I have a life, Sherry.

> LULU *returns.*

That was quick. Where is this mystery fulla?

LULU: He had to run off. But not to worry. You all get to meet him at rehearsals with Miss Esther. He's really looking forward to it.

MILO: Rehearsal?

LULU: The debutante.

QUEENIE: It's not that special.

LULU: Oh, it will be.

CHERYL: It's usually a colonial thing, you know, for rich white folks in high society.

LULU: Now we get to do it too. We dress up in white gowns and we make our grand entrance at the ball.

QUEENIE: As for me, I'm going by myself, out of protest.

MILO: Is that even allowed?

QUEENIE: Yes.

LULU: [*annoyed*] No.

QUEENIE: That's why it's called a protest.

LULU: Technically, the debutante is a protest. You're protesting a protest?

QUEENIE: If it means I get to do it on my own, then yes.

LULU: At the end the evening, we all get to dance.

QUEENIE: Sherry, you don't have a partner yet. You should ask Emilio to go.

LULU: That sounds like a great idea!

MILO: Oh no, not me.

CHERYL: Why not?

MILO: I'm not the best when it comes to dancing.

LULU: I'll teach you.

MILO: Maybe.

> MILO *gets up out of his seat.* CHERYL *stands with him.*

I really should get going too.

CHERYL: You know, you really don't have to leave.

QUEENIE: Yeah, we just got here.

MILO: It's okay … umm … thanks for the talk. I'm glad we ran into each other.

CHERYL: Yeah, same.

MILO: Maybe we can do it again soon.

CHERYL: Yeah, I'd like that.

MILO: Great. Girls, always a pleasure. We'll talk soon.

CHERYL: Okay.

MILO: Okay. Ciao.

QUEENIE: Ciao!

MILO *exits.* CHERYL *watches as he leaves.* LULU *and* QUEENIE *sit there looking at her.*

CHERYL: What?

QUEENIE: 'Maybe we can do it again soon.'

CHERYL *goes back to the table.*

CHERYL: Stop it.

QUEENIE: Stop what?

CHERYL: I know what you're thinking, and the answer is no.

QUEENIE: How do you know that I'm thinking that?

LULU: What is she thinking?

CHERYL: She thinks I like Milo.

LULU: You like Milo?!

CHERYL: No, I'm not saying I like—I'm saying that Queenie—

QUEENIE: I didn't say anything.

LULU: What happened to Michael? Did something happen to Michael?

CHERYL: No. Michael is fine. We're fine …

QUEENIE: Sherry, I've been your friend for too long to know when you like someone.

CHERYL: I don't like …

LULU: Milo, his name is Milo.

CHERYL: Milo. I do not like Milo … He was there, that's all. Nothing more. I love Michael. I am in love with Michael.

LULU: And Michael is thousands of miles away.

CHERYL: He's not dead, Lulu.

LULU: No, no, that's not what I mean.

QUEENIE: No. of course not. It's just …

CHERYL: What?

QUEENIE: It's nice to see you smile again.

CHERYL: I have to go.

CHERYL *exits.*

LULU: She likes him.

QUEENIE: Oh, without a doubt.

SCENE SIX: THERE IS SOMETHING ON YOUR MIND

Great Buckingham Street.

Redfern.

CHERYL *enters her room. She goes over to the box of letters sitting on her bed. She pulls out a stack of letters and begins opening them.* MICHAEL *enters.*

MICHAEL: April fifth, 1965. Cheryl-Lee. Oh, how I miss to say your name, to hear your voice, to see your smile. It's quiet nights like this, when I miss you the most. I look up at to stars to see anything remotely familiar to me, but the stars are different on this side of the world. Each night as I fall asleep, I picture you—

> CHERYL *drops the letter and picks up another.*

April twenty-ninth, Sherry—

> *And another.*

May fourteenth, 1965. There's this memory that keeps flooding back to me. The last summer together before I left. I think we must have spent the entire summer at the river that year. Perched under the shaded trees, the afternoon sun kissing our cool skin. You wrapped up in my arms—

> *She picks another letter.*

June first. I got another one of your letters—

> *And another.*

June twenty-ninth, 1965. I'll build it on a little piece of land, you know, not far from the river. A place where we can raise a family. Three. Two boys, and a little girl. She'll be just like you. Smart, beautiful, and a smile that lights up the room. We'll name her something sweet, like Rose or Violet because they remind me of you. I always think about you. You and everyone back home, my parents—

> *And another one.*

September eighth, 1965. Has it almost been a year? A whole year and it hasn't gotten any easier being away from—

CHERYL *starts flipping through the letters until she finds the one she's looking for.*

Hoping I get to see you all again. I love you. Yours truly, Michael.

CHERYL *drops the letter.* MICHAEL *exits.*

SCENE SEVEN: STUBBORN KIND OF FELLOW

Great Buckingham Street.

ERNIE *enters. Nervous. Fighting with himself every step he makes. He pulls out a letter from his back pocket and looks at it.*

ERNIE: I'm going to do it. I'm just gonna give it to her. I'll give it to her and say …

He stops.

What am I doing?

He turns back and stops.

How about … I leave it there. Yeah, I drop it off—what's the harm in that? She's not even home. You can talk to her? Yeah and what am I gonna say, huh? You can tell her? I'm not getting into this. It's all in the letter. The letter for … her. I should go home. Right. I should turn around and leave.

QUEENIE *enters in a rush. She's visibly upset. She reaches into her purse, trying to fish for her keys.*

QUEENIE: Where is it?!
ERNIE: Queenie?

QUEENIE *looks up startled but notices it's* ERNIE.

QUEENIE: Oh, it's you. What are you doing here?

ERNIE *pockets the letter.*

ERNIE: I was going to pop in to see Sherry.
QUEENIE: I don't think she's home.
ERNIE: Yeah, right, I had a feeling about that. You know where she is?
QUEENIE: I don't know, Palms?
ERNIE: Is that where you're going?
QUEENIE: What is with the questions?

ERNIE: What?

QUEENIE: All these questions, talking to me like I'm some sort of a witness. I don't know, maybe. I'll find out when I get there.

ERNIE: So you are going there then?

QUEENIE: What's it to you?

ERNIE: Fine, don't tell me then.

> ERNIE *begins to walk away but stops and turns to* QUEENIE.

You know what?

QUEENIE: What?

ERNIE: Why are you so stubborn?

QUEENIE: I'm stubborn?

ERNIE: Yes, you're stubborn. All you had to do is tell me, that's all. But it's never easy with you, is it? I ask you a question and it's like pulling teeth, because people have to do backflips around you, just to get an answer out of you.

QUEENIE: Maybe some people don't deserve an answer, you ever thought of that?

ERNIE: This is hopeless. Look, just tell Sherry I was looking for her, okay?

QUEENIE: Why don't you tell her yourself.

ERNIE: Just tell her.

QUEENIE: Fine. God damn it!

> *The purse drops, spilling some of her belongings onto the ground. She sits, defeated, trying to hold back tears.* ERNIE *approaches the house.*

ERNIE: Need any help?

QUEENIE: Not now, Ernest, I'm not in the mood.

ERNIE: Is everything alright?

QUEENIE: Everything is amazing.

ERNIE: You sure?

QUEENIE: Of course. It's a great day when you get to work and find out that your position has been terminated.

ERNIE: What?

QUEENIE: I got fired.

ERNIE: You're not gonna do anything about it?

QUEENIE: To be honest, I haven't thought that far ahead. I've been a bit pre-occupied with receiving the news that I've been fired. What is there to do?

ERNIE: Anything.

QUEENIE: Really? All that time spent in university and that's the best you can come up with. 'Anything.'

QUEENIE *takes a deep breath.*

It's been a hard day. Agh, and it's the same everywhere, isn't it?! Whether it's a factory in the city or the station back home. Mission managers, they're everywhere. And I worked hard too, I was on the rise there. Thinking of promoting me, you know? It was right there in front of me and now it's all gone.

ERNIE: What happened?

QUEENIE: I was late. One time, the one time I missed the bus. I got there, and they fired me on the spot, no questions asked.

ERNIE: But you're late all the time, though.

QUEENIE: Not to work, I'm not. No matter where we go, they treat us all the same. At this point I might as well take that nine-hour bus ride back home to Walgett.

ERNIE *straightens his shoulders.*

ERNIE: What's your boss's name?

QUEENIE: Mr Miller.

ERNIE: He still there?

QUEENIE: He should be.

ERNIE: I'll be back.

ERNIE *begins to leave.*

QUEENIE: Wait, where are you going?

ERNIE: I'm gonna pay Mr Miller a little visit.

QUEENIE: And do what?

ERNIE: We got to fight this.

QUEENIE: I don't need you to save me, Ernie.

ERNIE: You can take them to court, you can hold them accountable and get your—

QUEENIE: Why? It's not gonna change anything. They do this to us all the time.

ERNIE: That's not a life to settle on.

QUEENIE: But it's the life we have right now.

ERNIE: Queenie.

QUEENIE *begins to collect her belongings off the ground.*

Queenie!

QUEENIE: What?! What? Has it ever crossed your mind that maybe I don't want to do it? Our lives are hard enough without fighting every damn day to stay here. People like me can't barge into any office and demand respect. You can be the hardest and smartest worker in the room and they'll still treat you like dirt. It won't matter. What if I did do something about it, be like you and marched down there to give Mr Wilson a piece of my mind? Then what? No matter what I say, it's not going to change his decision about me or any of us. I've lost my job but I'm not willing to lose my dignity begging a white man to reconsider. I'm tired of fighting them, to be seen, to be wanted and, for once, I want someone to want me without me having to ask. I'll look for another job.

ERNIE: Let me represent you.

QUEENIE *laughs.*

I'm serious. I'm good. I can do it, I can help you.

QUEENIE: I told you, I don't need your help.

QUEENIE *picks up her purse and goes back to the doorstep and begins searching.*

ERNIE: What are you doing?

QUEENIE: I can't find my house keys.

QUEENIE *gives up and sits back on the step.*

Maybe I'll just stay out here forever. I can set up camp and stay here till I die.

ERNIE: Hey, hey, hey. None of that now.

QUEENIE: It's true.

ERNIE: You're being dramatic.

QUEENIE *screws up her face as* ERNIE *goes and sits next to her on the step. He reaches into his pocket and pulls out a handkerchief and hands it to* QUEENIE. *She takes the handkerchief.*

I'm not saying you have to do anything about it now. Just know I'm always here to help when you're in need. No matter what.

QUEENIE: Why are you nice to me all of a sudden?

ERNIE: I'm sure the last thing you need from me is a lecture.

QUEENIE: You're not wrong.

> *Beat.* QUEENIE *smiles but realises who she's smiling at.* QUEENIE *sees the letter in* ERNIE'*s hand.*

You want me to give that to Sherry?

ERNIE: Huh?

QUEENIE: The letter. It's for her, right? From Michael.

ERNIE: Right.

QUEENIE: Well, come on.

> ERNIE *clears his throat.*

ERNIE: It's okay, I'll give it to her later.

QUEENIE: You know, I've had such an awful day, it'll be nice to give someone some good news. So, you can give me the letter.

ERNIE: No, no, no.

> ERNIE *gets up and pockets the letter.*

QUEENIE: Ernest, if it's for Sherry, don't you think she should have it?

ERNIE: It's okay, I'll give it to her later.

QUEENIE: Ernie.

ERNIE: It's fine.

QUEENIE: Just give me the letter.

ERNIE: No.

QUEENIE: What's going on with you?

ERNIE: Why does anything need to be going on?

QUEENIE: Is it Sherry? Is there something wrong with Sherry?

ERNIE: Is there—I don't know. Actually, that's what I wanted to check—to check on that. See if she's okay. That's why I came here, in the first place. No other reason. I came to see Sherry and then I saw you and you were upset and I wanted to help.

QUEENIE: Right.

ERNIE: The offer is on the table, if you want me to help you with all that—that work stuff. It could make things a little easier. It seems like you need the help. Only if you like.

ERNIE *looks down and spots the key.*

Look, some good news.

ERNIE *hands* QUEENIE *her key.*

Now you don't have to break any windows. You can use the door because now you have the key.

QUEENIE: You sure you're alright?

ERNIE: Perfect.

ERNIE *turns and quickly leaves, beating himself up as he goes.*

SCENE EIGHT: AND I LOVE HER

CHERYL *continues to read each letter.* QUEENIE *enters, carrying a bag of tomatoes. She's relieved to see* CHERYL *sitting on her bed.*

QUEENIE: Great, you're home. You've been here the entire time?

CHERYL: Yeah, why?

QUEENIE: No reason.

QUEENIE: Let me tell you, I had a day.

CHERYL *waits.*

CHERYL: You gonna tell me?

QUEENIE: I don't want to get into it.

CHERYL: What's with the tomatoes?

QUEENIE: Dave, I asked him to help us out with food this week, since he got paid, so he went and brought me a bag of tomatoes. What am I gonna do with a bag of tomatoes?

QUEENIE *goes and lays on the bed.*

Ernie was looking for you.

CHERYL: When?

QUEENIE: Not too long ago. I think he was dropping one of Michael's letters off to you.

CHERYL: Where is it?

QUEENIE: He still has it.

CHERYL *places a letter into the shoebox.*

Tell me, what did Michael say in that sweet letter of yours? I need to hear something nice after the disaster of a day I had.

The girls sit in silence, as CHERYL *flips through her box of letters.*

He's a strange one.

CHERYL: Who?

QUEENIE: Ernie.

CHERYL: And you're only realising that now?

QUEENIE: I mean he's always been strange, but today, something was off. I got home, after the worst day of my life, because I got fired—

CHERYL: Fired?! What do you mean 'fired'? I can't be the only one paying for—

QUEENIE: Please, Sherry, can we focus on what's important? Me. I get home and he was there, for some stupid reason—I'm guessing to see you. But, I don't know, he wasn't his stupid self. He was … sweet. I mean, after I told him about being fired and he gave me his handkerchief. And you know what he said? That he reckons—get this—that he wanted to represent me, if I decided to take it further. How crazy is that? Trust me. It's crazy.

CHERYL: No surprise there, since he likes you and all.

QUEENIE *goes quiet.*

Very quiet.

QUEENIE: No, what? No! I'm just thinking about what I should make with these tomatoes. You like soup?

QUEENIE *gets up and begins pacing.*

What did you just say to me? Before? Say that again.

CHERYL: Ernie likes you.

QUEENIE: What?

CHERYL: How can you miss it? Oh yeah, Ernie has had a thing for you for as long as you've known each other.

QUEENIE *begins laughing.*

QUEENIE: Don't be stupid. He's a torment.

CHERYL: Queenie.

QUEENIE: Since when, exactly?

CHERYL: Since …

QUEENIE: No, no, don't tell me, I don't want to know.

CHERYL: I might be wrong, and it's simply nothing.

QUEENIE: But …

CHERYL: But … I know my brother, and Ernie doesn't fight like that with anyone and, for some reason / he loves fighting with you.

QUEENIE: Sherry! No! Stop it!

CHERYL: What is the big deal?

QUEENIE: This changes everything. Why did you tell me that, Sherry? How am I supposed to act around him, now that I know this?

CHERYL: Come on, Queenie, he's the same Ernie as before.

QUEENIE: No he's not, he's not the same Ernie that would pick fights with me every chance he gets. Ugh! You don't get it, Sherry.

CHERYL: What's not to get? You don't like hearing that someone likes you.

QUEENIE: No one likes hearing that someone might have feelings for them when they're not ready to hear it.

CHERYL: Why not?

QUEENIE: No one likes me like that, okay! No one has ever liked me like that.

Beat.

CHERYL: Queenie—

QUEENIE: I'm serious.

CHERYL: You don't really believe that, do you?

QUEENIE: Yes. Who wants to be with this? No matter what room I walk in, I'm constantly being reminded that I'm not enough or, better yet, that I'm too much. I talk too much. I'm too loud, too headstrong, too stubborn, too black. And there's no winning in the end, no matter what I do. And I get it. I'm not like those white women in the magazines, or some famous Hollywood actress from the picture shows. I'll never be like those women. Even if Ernie did want to be with someone like me, I know one day it'll be too much for him. I will be too much for him.

CHERYL: You don't know that.

QUEENIE: But I do.

CHERYL: Queenie, you are and will always be beautiful.

QUEENIE: You don't have to, Sherry—

CHERYL: Look at me. For as long as I've known you, rooms light up every time you walk in. How many times on our nights out we see these fellas flock towards you? I watch how these men look at you. You are so much more than what this world is showing you. You don't need to be like those women in the magazines or picture shows. You're wonderful. Don't let anyone make you feel anything otherwise.

QUEENIE: You think?

CHERYL: Us little Aboriginal girls can do whatever we want, and we do it with poise and style. And if people don't like us being who we are—to quote the famous Queenie Rivers—'Let them be jealous.' If you don't, you're gonna end up looking sour like Helen Peterson.

QUEENIE: Don't you dare say that to me.

> QUEENIE *raises her fist.* CHERYL *laughs.* LULU *enters.*

LULU: Oh, it's good to be home. Factory hours is a lot different than I'm used to.

CHERYL: Come, sit. We're talking about Helen Peterson.

LULU: Oooh remember what she did to you, Sherry, in the bathroom that one time.

CHERYL: To you too, Lulu.

QUEENIE: I hate her.

CHERYL: Queenie!

QUEENIE: It's true, after what she did to you, Lulu, I want nothing to do with her.

LULU: Oh, that? That was nothing.

QUEENIE: Lulu, she called you an uptown nigger and wanted to offer you out on the street.

LULU: Yeah, but I don't think she really meant it.

QUEENIE: I remember. I came into the bathroom, you two standing there—in front of me. And as soon as I heard those words come out of her mouth. I was ready to go at her. I was like, 'Listen here, you little black dog—'

LULU: Aye.

QUEENIE: 'Don't you think we deal with enough in this world without having to tear each other down? Call us whatever you want, it's not like we haven't heard it all before but us, here, we're good. We're not gonna dress, talk or carry ourselves any different to fit into your idea of what "black" is.' And that's what I said.

CHERYL: You didn't say that.

QUEENIE: I did.

CHERYL: We were all there. Lulu was the one that said that.

QUEENIE: I'm pretty sure it was me.

> *They laugh and settle in. Music is heard in the distance. The girls listen to the music.*

> LULU *sings the fourth verse of 'And I Love Her' by The Beatles.*

I got fired today.

LULU: Fired?! Queenie, why didn't you tell me? I was at work with you today.

QUEENIE: You were busy.

LULU: What are you gonna do about it?

QUEENIE: I'm thinking about taking them to court or, better yet, fight Mr Miller outside the factory.

LULU: You should do it.

QUEENIE: Fight Mr Miller?

CHERYL: No.

> QUEENIE *thinks about it.*

QUEENIE: Nah, I can't do that, can I? No, really, can I? Can you imagine me in court being all lawyerly? I object, this white man took my land and took my job away from me. And I want them both back now!

LULU: Ask Ernie if he can help you? He's really good at that stuff.

CHERYL: I'm sure he is.

LULU: Oh, he'll be happy to help you out. He did that for Helen Peterson that one time.

QUEENIE: When?

CHERYL: Calm down, it had to do something with helping her father and this deal with a car. She just wanted to be sure it wasn't dodgy.

QUEENIE: Yeah, but why does it have to be her?

LULU: Why do you care?

QUEENIE: I don't.

> *Beat.*

Come on, Lulu.

LULU: Where are we going?

QUEENIE: My room. / I need to pick out an outfit for my birthday. I need your help.

LULU: My room too.

>CHERYL *laughs.*

Don't you laugh at me, Cheryl-Lee. I want to look good. Come on, Lulu.

>QUEENIE *exits with* LULU. CHERYL *folds the letter from* MICHAEL *and slips it into her shoebox of belongings and puts it away. She exits. The city is quiet, and we hear jazz music being played from the house across the street.*

SCENE NINE: FRIDAY ON MY MIND

Redfern Park.

The streets are quiet and dark, with a few soft street lamps glowing around. MILO *enters. He waits for a bit before lighting a cigarette.* CHERYL *rushes in, trying to gather herself.*

CHERYL: Hey.

>MILO *turns to see* CHERYL. *He exhales.*

MILO: Hey.

CHERYL: You've been waiting out here long?

MILO: Not too long. You run here?

CHERYL: No.

>CHERYL *touches her cheek.* MILO *takes a drag from his cigarette.*

It's a warm night.

MILO: Yeah, it's pretty warm. More than usual, I guess.

CHERYL: It's just you?

MILO: For now.

CHERYL: Ernie's not here yet?

MILO: He doesn't seem to be.

CHERYL: Good. I mean, it's no surprise, Ernie being late. Queenie had an emergency last-minute outfit change herself. Emergency. I know she wanted everything to be perfect tonight. For her birthday.

MILO: And you're not there to help her?

CHERYL: It'll be fine. She'll find another outfit, put it on and realise the first outfit was the right one all along.

MILO: You know a lot, don't you?

CHERYL: I know Queenie.

MILO *offers* CHERYL *a cigarette.*

Oh, no, I can't. You should stop that though. I read they're not the best for you.

MILO *takes another drag.*

MILO: Is that so? Why all of a sudden your interest in my health?

CHERYL: Who said I'm interested?

MILO *takes a drag of his cigarette and puts it out. Music plays from one of the houses.*

Can I ask you something?

MILO: Sure.

CHERYL: You don't have to, if you don't want to. Talk about it, I mean …

MILO: We can talk about it if you actually get around to asking me the question.

CHERYL: Right. What's university like? I know it might sound silly of me to ask—

MILO: You have your brother, why not ask him?

CHERYL: Because I'm asking you. You like it? It's not like I haven't thought about it before. I grew up with a father that taught us kids two things. One: 'that getting an education was important'. But I've been thinking about it more and more recently. About everything, actually. Take Ernie … ever since he stepped foot into that school, he just grew into this new person: strong, determined. Don't get me wrong, he's stubborn as hell but everything shifted for him. The way he can see his life right there in front of him, knowing exactly where he wants to go. It might be the change I need. I can't spend the rest of my life waiting on letters that don't end up coming.

MILO: Does Ernie know you're thinking of going … Shouldn't this be something you share with him?

CHERYL: Probably.

MILO: What are you waiting for? I mean, when it comes to decisions like this, the only one who's holding you back is you.

CHERYL *watches* MILO *carefully.*

What?

CHERYL: I haven't quite figured you out yet.

MILO: Funny, I can say the same thing to you.

CHERYL: You're too nice.

MILO: Right.

CHERYL: It's true, you're too nice. I mean, there has to be something underneath all this. You must have secrets, a past you're afraid to talk about. And yet you say nothing.

MILO: What if there's nothing to say?

Beat.

What do you want to know?

CHERYL: Family?

MILO: I have a mother, whom I love dearly and insist I visit three times a week. A father that rarely keeps in touch. And one day I want to go back and visit the village where my mum was born.

CHERYL: Where is that?

MILO: A small village, east of Naples.

CHERYL: I bet it's lovely there.

Music plays from one of the houses. CHERYL *takes a moment and listens for the music echoing through the quiet streets.*

MILO: I don't think you can get this anywhere else but in the city.

They listen. CHERYL *starts humming along knowingly.*

CHERYL: You don't dance, right?

MILO: Me? No.

CHERYL: How come?

MILO: Don't like it.

CHERYL: You don't like to dance?

MILO: Not in front of people, no. I'm no Fred Astaire.

CHERYL: No one is Fred Astaire. I'm sure you can dance if you really gave it a shot.

CHERYL *starts dancing.*

It's fun.

MILO: I'm okay.

CHERYL: No-one around.

MILO *begins dancing.* CHERYL *tries not to laugh.*

MILO: I'm stopping. / Before I make a complete fool of myself.
CHERYL: I'm sorry. I'm sorry, I didn't mean to laugh.

    Beat.

  Here, let me help.

    CHERYL *goes to help* MILO.

MILO: What are you doing?
CHERYL: I'm teaching you how to dance.
MILO: I know how to dance. I just don't like to do it.
CHERYL: Okay. Show me then.

    MILO *takes* CHERYL*'s hand and steps into her.*

MILO: Did your dad teach you how to dance?

    CHERYL *looks at him confused.*

CHERYL: What do you mean?
MILO: You said your dad taught you two things. I was wondering what
    the second thing was.
CHERYL: He also taught me how to throw a mean right hook.

    They begin swaying.

    MILO *spins* CHERYL.

MILO: You asked anyone to the debutante yet?
CHERYL: Yeah, I have.
MILO: Who's the lucky guy?
CHERYL: Paul Ryan.
MILO: Paul Ryan?
CHERYL: You know him?
MILO: Met him a couple of times with Ernie. He's …
CHERYL: I know, I know, he can be a bit …
MILO: Boring, dull. A real stick in the mud.
CHERYL: He's not—
MILO: He is. Come on, you can't deny that the man can be—
CHERYL: He's lovely and I'm honoured to have him as my partner to
    the debutante.
MILO: I'm sorry, I didn't mean to be so …
CHERYL: It's okay. I mean he's no Rodney Roberts but there was no-one
    else that would have me in such short notice.

MILO: You could have asked me.

CHERYL *giggles.*

What?

CHERYL: You said no, remember? But I'm surprised someone like you is even thinking about a debutante. Especially one like this.

MILO: Someone like me?

CHERYL: Yeah … Aren't you like Ernie?

MILO: You think I'm like Ernie?

CHERYL: It's all about law and legislation with you lot, right?

MILO: Sometimes.

CHERYL: Like I said, an Aboriginal debutante ball wouldn't interest people like you.

MILO: How do you know? I have many interests.

CHERYL: Like what?

MILO: Like you. You interest me.

CHERYL *and* MILO *hold each other's gaze.* ERNIE *enters, carrying a newspaper.* CHERYL *tries to gather herself.*

ERNIE: Hey, you've been waiting long?

MILO: Just got here.

ERNIE: Okay, good. Here.

ERNIE *hands the paper to* CHERYL *to read.*

Read this.

CHERYL: 'The main issue in the forthcoming Federal Referendum is in the need to remove two constitutional barriers to further advance the Aboriginal people towards full rights.' Isn't this what you want?

ERNIE: Parts. But amending the constitution won't solve the real problems we face.

CHERYL: It's a start, right? We have to begin somewhere.

ERNIE: We've *been* doing the work and we all know these white folks aren't gonna do shit to help us unless there's something in for them. Conditions. Nah, it's up to us and us alone, taking things into our own hands and fighting back. Just like in America with Dr King and Malcolm X, teaching mob that they can stand up for themselves, that they don't have to put up with this system anymore. That very system that forced us to hate ourselves. Their sheer objective to turn us extinct. Yet we're still here. Still standing strong. And we're all coming together to fight this. Just think what would happen if we step into this with both feet. Maybe we will become citizens, maybe the war will end, and everyone can come home. The possibilities are endless right now. We can do anything, and it's happening right in front of our very eyes!

QUEENIE: [*offstage*] Woo! I'm with you, Ernest!

QUEENIE *and* LULU *enter.*

LULU: Very supportive.

QUEENIE: I can't be supportive?

LULU: Not to Ernie.

CHERYL: Finally.

QUEENIE: Yes, I am here.

CHERYL: I see you went with the first outfit.

QUEENIE: I did!

LULU: [*to* CHERYL] Don't get me started.

MILO: Happy birthday, Queenie.

MILO *hands* QUEENIE *a bottle of wine.*

QUEENIE: Oh, vino. Thank you, Emilio. Like my hair? Lulu did it, gave me extra body.

LULU: Can you quit touching it, you're gonna make it go flat.

QUEENIE: Okay! I won't touch it. You weren't waiting long, I hope?

CHERYL: Not at all.

MILO: Ernie was sharing news about the referendum.

LULU: I read about that.

QUEENIE: Me too!

LULU *shoots* QUEENIE *a confused look at her excitement in politics.*

LULU: Big things are happening. Today I was reading about—

QUEENIE: Okay, okay, okay, I'm sure it's all happening, but for one night, can we not talk about politics? This is your night off because this is *my* night. And since I'm the birthday girl, I have a few things to say.

LULU: Here we go.

QUEENIE: First of all, I want to thank Ernest. Because of you I got my job back. I stood up to the man and stuck it to him.

ERNIE: I don't think you ever said thank you to me before.

LULU: Don't get used to it.

QUEENIE: Hey, hey, hey, no, things are different. I want to show my appreciation. I've never done something like that before.

CHERYL: Be nice to Ernie?

QUEENIE: Shut up! I pulled myself together and we marched to that man's office and took him head on. And we won! I did that, with the help of Ernest, of course. Ernest, I promise to listen more to your endless rants and hope I get to be as knowledgeable as you one day. Should we open the wine?

LULU: They're uniting.

CHERYL: It's sweet. When do we ever see these two find a middle ground?

LULU: Let's see how long it'll last.

QUEENIE: Jesus, Ernest!

ERNIE: What?!

QUEENIE: Will you watch where you're going? You stepped on my foot.

ERNIE: Well, if you move your big foot, I'll have somewhere to step.

> QUEENIE *and* ERNIE *continue arguing and* LULU *trying her best to break them up.* OFFICER ROBINSON *enters. Everyone stops.*

ROBINSON: Evening. We're looking for a man by the name of David Roberts.

> *He looks at everyone. He points to* ERNIE.

You. Come here.

> ERNIE *steps forward.*

You got a name?

> *Beat.*

Did you hear me? I said do you have a name?

ERNIE: Yeah.

ROBINSON: Well, are you gonna tell me your name or not?

> ERNIE *stays quiet.*

There's been a few robberies, some breaking and entries happening around here.

ERNIE: What's your point?

ROBINSON: Where were you Wednesday night between seven p.m. and seven a.m.?

ERNIE: Seriously?

ROBINSON: Answer the question.

> *Nothing.*

I'm gonna ask you one more time. What is your name and where were you on Wednesday night?

> ERNIE *refuses to answer.*

Alright, turn around / and put your hands behind your back.

ERNIE: What?

> *Everyone jumps in, speaking over each other.*

CHERYL: Officer, there's some mistake.

QUEENIE: He hasn't done anything.

LULU: We live right over there.

QUEENIE: Don't tell him that.

ROBINSON: Enough! That's a nice bottle you got there. What are we celebrating? Tsk, tsk, tsk. Drinking in public. Don't you blacks know better than that?

> *Everyone goes quiet.*

Now, turn around and put your hands behind your head.

ERNIE: Hang on, you can't—

ROBINSON: Turn around.

> ERNIE *begins to slowly turn around, putting his hands behind his back while the girls object, as* OFFICER ROBINSON *reaches for his handcuffs.*

CHERYL: Don't do this. He can't do this.

> MILO *quickly tries to step in between* ERNIE *and* OFFICER ROBINSON.

MILO: Whoa, whoa, whoa. Hey, let's just stop for a second.

> OFFICER ROBINSON *stops.*

Look … we don't have to do this.

> OFFICER ROBINSON *grins at* MILO.

ROBINSON: Milo. Is that you? What are you doing over this way?

MILO: Good to see you too, Benny. Listen, you got the wrong man. I know for a fact that you're not looking for him.

ROBINSON: And how do you know he's not the guy I'm looking for? You know this one?

MILO: Yeah, I know him.

ROBINSON: You don't say. You know, you're the last person I thought would be friends with a black.

QUEENIE: Black?!

CHERYL: Let's just leave.

ROBINSON: No-one leaves until I say they can, you hear me?

MILO: And you're the last person I thought would be wearing a uniform, trying to uphold the law. Tell me Benny, how it going for you?

OFFICER ROBINSON *chuckles.*

ROBINSON: I see you're still the same smartarse.

MILO: It keeps me busy.

ROBINSON: I'm sure it does. Tell me, which one of the gins are you with?

ERNIE: Hey.

ROBINSON: You got something to say boy?

OFFICER ROBINSON *steps in close to* CHERYL *for a better look.*

Must be this one, hey? You're right, Milo, she is a pretty one. I had my suspicion you liked your meat a little darker. [*To* CHERYL] I'm not one to say that to your kind. But you are quite a looker. I'll watch out for this fulla though, if I were you.

CHERYL: I think I can make my own mind up on that one.

ROBINSON: Ooh, fiery one too. I can see why Milo likes you. [*To* MILO] It must nice having this entire new life. Long, long away from what we got up to back in the day. Look at you now, out here, making nice with a bunch of no-good blacks. Tell me, Milo, you think any one of these gonna stick around after they find out about you? The real you?

CHERYL: What is he talking about?

ROBINSON: You don't know?

CHERYL: Milo, what is he talking about?

ROBINSON: Yeah, Milo, share with the rest of us, the little adventures you would get up to.

MILO: I don't know what you're talking about.

ROBINSON: Sure you do. Try.

> MILO *doesn't answer.*

No? What, you can't speak to a friend about the good days? Then allow me to refresh your memory. Remember when you beat the shit out of that boy? He ended up in the hospital, all because of you.

MILO: I know what you're doing.

ROBINSON: Do you now?

MILO: He's not the man you're looking for.

ROBINSON: I'm just doing my job and your 'friend' there fits the description. On that alone, gives me enough to drag him to the station for questioning. That could change if he gives me his name.

MILO: He doesn't need to give you his name.

ROBINSON: You his lawyer?

MILO: No.

ROBINSON: Then why should I give a fuck about what you think?

MILO: As an old friend then, just let this all go.

ROBINSON: I would love to, but can't. Protocol.

QUEENIE: I've had enough of this. I'm going.

ROBINSON: Now, wait right there, little lady. You haven't gotten my permission to go.

ERNIE: She don't need your permission.

> *Beat.*

ROBINSON: It seems like every week I see you people coming to the city in droves. You step off those trains with your suitcases. Coming into my town and running rampant through my streets without a care in the world about the destruction you leave behind. Nothing but a bunch of lowlife mutts.

ERNIE: That's rich coming from you.

> ERNIE *steps forwards but* CHERYL *blocks him, wedging herself between* OFFICER ROBINSON *and* ERNIE.

CHERYL: Officer, this isn't the man you're looking for—

ERNIE: No, you don't have to explain anything to him. The man wants to talk, so we should let him talk. Let's hear what he has to say.

ROBINSON: None of you should be out here.

ERNIE: Is that all you've got?

CHERYL: Leave it, Ernie.

ROBINSON: We have a name. Ernie. Yeah, yeah, now I remember you. It's always good to put a name to face. We get a visit from you down at the station a fair bit. If you're lucky, maybe I'll get to hear that pretty little cry of yours again.

CHERYL: Okay, you got a name. He's clearly not the one you're looking for. Let's go.

ROBINSON: Not quite yet. I'm not done with you.

ERNIE: I've had enough of cunts like you thinking they run these streets. You know that badge you got? It's nothing. It means nothing. You can walk around here high and mighty all you want. You'll still be nothing.

ROBINSON: You threatening me boy? You're all criminals in my book. What can you do, anyways? Who's gonna stop me? I can even take one of these black bitches down to the station and have my way with them while you watch. What do you think of that … boy?

ERNIE: I told you, I'm not your fucking boy!

ERNIE *swings and punches* OFFICER ROBINSON. OFFICER ROBINSON *grabs* ERNIE, *slamming him on the ground, and begins handcuffing him.*

Get the fuck off me!

QUEENIE: Hey, get the fuck off him!

QUEENIE *goes to throw a punch but is stopped by* LULU.

LULU: Queenie, no.

CHERYL *freezes, watching as* OFFICER ROBINSON *grabs* QUEENIE *and* LULU.

[*to* OFFICER ROBINSON] You're hurting me.

MILO: [*to* CHERYL] Get out of here. Hurry. Go!

In the commotion, CHERYL *snaps out of it and runs off as* MILO *goes after the others.*

Lights out.

ACT TWO

SCENE TEN: DON'T WORRY BABY

Redfern backstreets.

CHERYL *runs in, looking behind to see if anyone was behind her. She stops to catch her breath.* CHERYL *waits for a moment, pacing, checking for any signs of police or the others. She jumps as* MILO *enters, out of breath.*

CHERYL: What are you doing? We have to go back!

MILO: We can't.

CHERYL: You left them?! Queenie and Lulu? They've never been …

MILO: Ernie is with them. He won't let anything happen.

CHERYL: What if they do something to him? What would happen then? He hit a fucking police officer!

MILO: Nothing is going to happen to him, okay? I won't let it.

CHERYL: The officer. You know him, right?

MILO: No. Look, it doesn't matter right now.

CHERYL: It means everything right now.

MILO: Benny is an asshole. You think I was any exception back there because I knew him?

> MILO *pulls out a cigarette and lights it. Silence.* MILO *takes a drag, shaking his head out of frustration.*

CHERYL: You should stop that.

> CHERYL *goes to leave but stops.*

They were black. That's what he was going on about. The boys, at the park. They were black boys, weren't they?

> MILO *doesn't answer.* CHERYL *goes to leave.*

Right.

MILO: Wait, Sherry, wait a minute, it wasn't like that.

CHERYL: Did Ernie know about this?

MILO: I didn't do what you're accusing me of doing.

CHERYL: And what am I accusing you of doing? That's why he was talking all that stuff about how we wouldn't stick around if we knew the truth about you, right?

MILO: And you believe him?! The same asshole that dragged Ernie off just now? You're going to believe a man like that?

Beat.

What do you want me to say? I didn't know any better back then and I wish I did. I was a stupid kid that hung out with pricks like him. I did things I'm not proud of, for people who I thought had my back. And I was wrong for it, I can admit that. I was wrong about them, like I was wrong about a lot of things, and if I could go back there and undo what I did, I would … but I can't.

CHERYL *walks away. She stops and looks up to the sky.*

CHERYL: I hate it here. I hate that I see my brother get dragged off by police again. I hate that we get punished for simply existing.

Beat.

I watch how they treat us. I watched how people like your friend there—

MILO: He's not my friend—

CHERYL: Whoever he is. A police officer that gets a kick from terrorising Aboriginal people. They can't help themselves but go on some sort of power trip as if it was some personal vendetta. Ernie speaks his mind and they beat him for it. I watch them. The words they use. I see it in their eyes, I look at them and see the hatred they have for him. Like daggers, wanting to cut him open and spill him out onto the pavement, right there in front of them. Just because they feel like it that day. It's ingrained in them to hate us, to hold power over us, and for what? Because you think you're better than us. You're more deserving of this place than us?

I watched how my parents, my grandparents, try and push back against a government that wants nothing more than to have them gone. Do you know how that feels? To grow and live in a country where you know that the majority of people here wished you were dead. Reminding us that their lives and this country would be better off without us existing here in the first place.

It doesn't matter, really. What do they know? They don't know us, and they don't want to know us. They don't want to know that we love dancing and we love to sing just like they do. That we have dreams to see the world. To work and own a home. To have a family, or to fall in love. Do they know that we want that too? God, what did we do to be treated this way? Ernie's right, it's easier for them to believe the lies. It's easier for them to hate us. What do they have to lose, right? They'll go about their day, and if we get in their way, they'll just keep kicking us down and hoping we don't get back up. And I'm sick of it. I mean … Aren't you tired of living like this? I know I am. I'm tired of all the hurting, I'm tired of seeing people around me hurt day after day here. But most of all I'm scared … I'm really scared that this is it for us.

Silence fills the dark night. MILO *watches* CHERYL *for a moment before stepping forward.*

MILO: You're bleeding.

CHERYL looks to see bloodstains her dress. MILO *goes to examine the wound.* CHERYL *winces.*

Did I hurt you?

CHERYL: Your hands are cold.

MILO: Shit, sorry.

MILO *tries to warm his hands up.*

CHERYL: First time? It's a lot different when they start singling you out.

MILO *pulls a handkerchief out and cleans the wound. He finishes by tying the handkerchief.*

MILO: How's that? That should hold up until you get home.

CHERYL: Thanks.

They hold each other's gazes for a moment. CHERYL *leans in and kisses* MILO *and he returns the kiss.* CHERYL *suddenly pulls away. Silence.*

MILO: Sherry, I didn't mean—

CHERYL: I'm sorry about that.

MILO: What?

CHERYL: Really, I shouldn't have done that.

MILO: It's alright, you don't have to—

CHERYL: No, no, no. It was completely … wrong of me. I'm sorry. I didn't mean to—

MILO: It wasn't just you—

CHERYL: I wasn't thinking … I—I um … I'm really sorry.

MILO: You don't have to apologise.

CHERYL: No, I do. I do, because this whole thing is …

MILO: What?

CHERYL: Wrong.

MILO: Wrong?

CHERYL: None of this should have happened in the first place.

> CHERYL *runs off.* MILO *stands there unsure what to do. He pulls out a cigarette, lights it and walks in the opposite direction.*

SCENE ELEVEN: WE GOT TO GET OUT OF THIS PLACE

Palms Milk Bar.

ERNIE, QUEENIE *and* LULU *enter the milk bar. They slide into a booth, exhausted.*

LULU: I don't think I'll ever go out again.

ERNIE: You can't say that. We can't let those dogs intimidate us. What they do around here is unlawful—

LULU: Ernie, can you get off your soap box for a second? If you haven't noticed, I spent last night locked up!

ERNIE: We all did.

LULU: I don't want to get into it.

ERNIE: We should talk about it.

LULU: I don't.

> CHERYL *enters.*

CHERYL: How did you go?

> CHERYL *looks at the bruise on* ERNIE's *face.*

Nice shiner you got there.

ERNIE: I've had worse.

CHERYL: Lulu?

LULU: Just some bruises.

CHERYL: I was really worried about you.

QUEENIE *stays silent, clearly upset.*

Say, let me buy you a milkshake.

QUEENIE *doesn't respond.*

You're not talking to me?

QUEENIE: No.

Silence.

LULU: I'm happy to get the milkshakes.

ERNIE: I'll help ya.

QUEENIE: If Cheryl's buying, I don't want one.

CHERYL: You got a problem, Queenie?

QUEENIE: Did you not see what happened to us last night?

LULU: Queenie.

CHERYL: No, it's okay, Lulu. Yeah I saw what happened.

QUEENIE: And where were you?

CHERYL: What?

QUEENIE: Where were you?

LULU: Maybe we should talk about this later.

QUEENIE: No, Sherry's a big girl. She can hear what I have to say now. She saw it all. And what did she do? She ran.

CHERYL: You know that's not what happened.

QUEENIE: Then tell me. Share with us what you did.

CHERYL: We're not doing this right now.

QUEENIE: You have other places to be than here?

CHERYL: It's not like that, Queenie.

QUEENIE: Then what is it?

CHERYL: I can't always be there, especially when Ernie wants to run his mouth!

ERNIE: I wasn't running my mouth.

CHERYL: You do it every time. I told you not every interaction has to end with a confrontation.

ERNIE: He approached us.

QUEENIE: They were going to grab him whether he opened his mouth or not.

CHERYL: What's your point?

QUEENIE: Aren't you angry?

CHERYL: Aren't I … What are you talking about, of course I'm angry.

QUEENIE: You sure about that?

CHERYL: Queenie, just because I'm not up at the station, screaming the place down—

QUEENIE: You should be—

CHERYL: Doesn't mean I'm not angry. I hate this just as much as you, but—

QUEENIE: But what?

> QUEENIE *gets up.*

CHERYL: You know what I saw last night. I've seen the same officers do the same thing every Friday and Saturday night.

QUEENIE: That doesn't make it right!

CHERYL: I'm not saying it was wrong or right.

ERNIE: No one is saying that.

QUEENIE: I am. It's wrong. And we're supposed to accept it. These officers, as soon as they put that uniform on, have this insane want for power. What are we waiting for? What will happen when they take it too far? One of us, or someone else, ends up dead in their custody? No, I won't have that. You know, the sickening thing about this is those very same officers that like to throw their weight around, throwing punches like it's some sort of sport to them— they'll get away with it. Every single one of them.

ERNIE: Something will be done. I know I've fucking had enough.

QUEENIE: And when will that happen?

CHERYL: You don't think I've been in those cells before? That I haven't sat on the cold concrete, bruises on my arms the next day?

QUEENIE: This isn't about you, Sherry! I got fired, I got arrested on my birthday week, me and Lulu are covered in bruises—

CHERYL: We're all going through something, Queenie, not just you.

QUEENIE: Don't talk down to me.

CHERYL: I'm not.

QUEENIE: You were just too busy with that Italian fulla.

ERNIE: With Milo?

CHERYL: It's nothing.

QUEENIE: Of course it's something. What would Michael think?

CHERYL: … You're mad at me, okay, be mad at me. But don't speak on things you know nothing about.

ERNIE: Come on, Sherry.

CHERYL: Last night was out of our control.

QUEENIE: And you ran off with Milo.

CHERYL: I didn't run.

QUEENIE: Yes, you did. He told you to run and you went 'how far?'

LULU: Okay, let's take a breath.

QUEENIE: I don't need to take a breath.

CHERYL: You have to know that I wanted to go back. To find you and Lulu—

QUEENIE: No, no, you don't bring Lulu into this.

CHERYL: Queenie, I'm sorry that / this has happened to you.

QUEENIE: Don't tell me you're sorry. Tell me you hate this, tell me you've had enough but don't stand there and tell me that you're sorry.

CHERYL: I'm here right now.

QUEENIE: Too little, too late.

> QUEENIE *storms off.* CHERYL *stands there in shock. She looks at* LULU *and* ERNIE. CHERYL *exits.* ERNIE *and* LULU *sit quietly.*

ERNIE: Should we go after them?

LULU: Give them a few hours to cool down. No one wants to be on the other end of Queenie's punches right now.

> *Pause.*

Ernie, can I ask you something?

ERNIE: Anything.

LULU: The first time you got grabbed and locked up, were you scared?

ERNIE: Yeah.

LULU: I don't understand. We've done nothing wrong. Last night we did nothing wrong. Queenie's right, these men with these badges think they have the right to treat people like that, like they're the law, and because they're the law they're exempted from any accountability.

ERNIE: Crazy things happen when you receive power. When you get it, you don't know what to do with it. But you know you'll do anything to hold on to it, even if it means attacking those more vulnerable than you.

LULU: How many times have you've been locked up like that? For what?

ERNIE: I hate to say it, but I'm pretty much used to it.

LULU: Is that it? You allow yourself to get used to it? The hate, the anger thrown at you day in and day out?

ERNIE: We become resilient to it. Knowing that whatever they do will not break our spirit. This fire in our belly that keeps telling us to keep going. I can't explain it, but maybe we're on the right track. These problems may not disappear completely overnight, but we could be heading in the right direction.

Beat.

I'm sorry, Lulu.

LULU: I guess we all have to experience it at least once in our lives.

ERNIE: It shouldn't be our rite of passage.

I've had my fair share of fighting and spent plenty of nights in those cages standing up for what's right. But last night, you shouldn't have been there, both you and Queenie.

LULU: I'm glad you were there with us though.

ERNIE: Always.

Beat.

I should go check on the girls. You're gonna be okay?

LULU: I'll get there.

ERNIE *begins to leave.*

LULU: Which one are you gonna see?

ERNIE *stops.*

ERNIE: Huh?

LULU: You're gonna see Queenie, right?

ERNIE: What do you mean?

LULU: A simple yes or no would do.

ERNIE *stands there, embarrassed.*

Ernie, I may be quiet, but I see everything.

ERNIE: Don't say anything, okay? I'm trying to figure it out.

LULU: I won't.

ERNIE *nods in agreement and begins to exit.*

ERNIE: Lulu … it's okay to be scared.

> LULU *gives* ERNIE *a small smile as he exits.* LULU *takes a moment. She sits in silence.*

SCENE TWELVE: WHATCHA GONNA DO ABOUT IT

Redfern Park.

QUEENIE *is sitting at a park bench, upset.* ERNIE *enters. He shrugs out of his coat and drapes it over* QUEENIE*'s shoulders.*

QUEENIE: What are you doing?
ERNIE: Thought you would be cold.

> ERNIE *takes a seat next to* QUEENIE.

You want to talk about it?
QUEENIE: There's nothing to talk about.

> QUEENIE *waits for* ERNIE *to say something.*

That's it?
ERNIE: What?
QUEENIE: That's all you're gonna say?
ERNIE: What do you want me to say?
QUEENIE: Nothing.
ERNIE: Then I'll say nothing.

> *Silence.*

QUEENIE: Just like that? No lecture.

> ERNIE *shakes his head no.*

ERNIE: None of that.
QUEENIE: What's the catch?
ERNIE: No catch. You don't want to talk about it. So, we don't have to talk about it.
QUEENIE: Okay.
ERNIE: Okay.

> *They sit in silence for a moment, looking around the park.*

There is something.

> QUEENIE *sighs loudly.*

QUEENIE: What happened to no talking?

ERNIE: Hear me out, will you? Sherry had mentioned you a couple of times to me. Told me she met a girl from up north at work. I think she was happy she had another friend here in the city. The night I met you, I was playing at the talent show with a few of the fellas. Sherry was running late as always. When I got off the stage to give her an earful, there you were. You barged into the room. Told me to 'wake up to myself and to leave her alone'. No one has ever done that to me before. But I knew in that moment, Sherry had found a good friend.

QUEENIE: Don't—

ERNIE: I know, I know, you don't want to talk about Sherry and we won't.

QUEENIE: Why do I have the feeling you're gonna talk about it more?

ERNIE: Because you need to know that we're all here for each other and last night was bad timing—

QUEENIE: Everything is bad timing here—

ERNIE: Sometimes we get into situations we should never be in. But at this moment in time, it's something we just have to deal with. You get that?

QUEENIE: It doesn't make it fair.

ERNIE: Is that what you want? Fair?

QUEENIE: Sometimes.

ERNIE: Then you wouldn't be Queenie. You wouldn't be this tough, loud—

QUEENIE: There better be a compliment somewhere in there.

ERNIE: Confident, loyal, beautiful person. All that other stuff is boring, and you don't want to be boring.

    QUEENIE *shakes her head.*

Life might not be fair, especially for us, but you said it once—it's the life we have right now. That doesn't mean it's going to be forever. We'll look back on this one day and see how far we've come, but until then we have to pick our fights.

QUEENIE: But you pick every fight you have. There's been times where you're even starting the fight.

ERNIE: Look, we're not talking about me right now.

QUEENIE: Yeah, but you said that—

ERNIE: What did I just say about picking fights?

QUEENIE: Okay.

ERNIE: Okay.

> *Beat.*

QUEENIE: You know, you're actually good at this talking stuff.

ERNIE: It's a good thing I don't shut up, huh?

QUEENIE: Sometimes.

> *Something shifts between them as they sit quietly next to each in silence.*

ERNIE: There's actually something I wanted to give you, for a while now.

QUEENIE: I know.

ERNIE: You know what?

QUEENIE: I know.

ERNIE: You know … What are you talking about?

QUEENIE: I know that you …

ERNIE: That I … what?

QUEENIE: That you like me.

> ERNIE *tries to cover his embarrassment with laughter.*

ERNIE: What?

QUEENIE: I know you like me.

ERNIE: Who—who—I mean, how, how do you know?

QUEENIE: Well …

ERNIE: Who said, who told you that I—

QUEENIE: Sherry told me.

ERNIE: Sherry told you, Sherry knows. She knows, and she told you. She said that I—

QUEENIE: That you like me.

> ERNIE *is silent.*

Ernest Johnson, I've never seen you lost for words before. I could get used to this.

> ERNIE *gets up.*

ERNIE: Ugh! You're so infuriating sometimes, do you know that?

QUEENIE: I'm infuriating? What about you?

ERNIE: My god, you're stubborn.

QUEENIE: Call me stubborn one more time. I dare you.

ERNIE: I come out here to do something nice. I helped you with your job! I tell you I like you, but it turns out, you knew all along.

QUEENIE: What?! You did not tell me you like me.

ERNIE: Yes, I did.

QUEENIE: No, you didn't, because I had to find out from your sister!

ERNIE: What about you, you like me?

QUEENIE: When?

ERNIE: Before.

QUEENIE: You need to be more specific.

ERNIE: At the beginning, when we first met.

QUEENIE: Oh, I had a crush when I first met you, no surprise there.

ERNIE: So you do like me.

QUEENIE: I *did* like you, there's a difference.

ERNIE: No there's not.

QUEENIE: Yes there is.

ERNIE: No there's not—

QUEENIE: We're not doing this.

> ERNIE *paces back and forth, frustrated.*

ERNIE: So, do you like me now?

QUEENIE: No … maybe.

ERNIE: Maybe?

QUEENIE: Yes. Maybe.

ERNIE: So whatcha gonna do about it?

QUEENIE: Who, me?!

ERNIE: Yes, you. No-one else is here but you. Tell me, what you are you gonna do about—

> QUEENIE *grabs* ERNIE*'s face and kisses him.*

QUEENIE: You wanna get out of here?

ERNIE: Now?

QUEENIE: Nah, later.

ERNIE: What?

QUEENIE: Yeah, now.

ERNIE: Sure.

> *They exit.*

SCENE THIRTEEN: OH DARLING

Great Buckingham Street.

CHERYL *sits on the steps of her house. She grabs the latest letter and opens it.* MICHAEL *enters.*

MICHAEL: I've been thinking … Dangerous, I know. Being away from home for so long, I find myself doing it a lot these days. Thinking about what's to come, it's the only thing that brings me some sort of comfort. Knowing there's a possible world where it might be better. Maybe. But I guess that all I can do is hope and dream. If it's even possible to do that, to hold on to a dream that seems so far away from me. Dreams of how I want to buy a house—I'll build it on a little piece of land, you know, not far from the river. A place where we can raise a family. Three. Two boys, and a little girl. She'll be just like you. Smart, beautiful, and a smile that lights up the room. We'll name her something sweet, like Rose or Violet because they remind me of you. I think about you a lot too. You and everyone back home, my parents. Hoping I get to see you all again, soon.

> MICHAEL *takes a seat at the end of the bed and looks up as if he's looking at the stars in the night sky.*

You ever think I made the right decision coming here? Knowing you, you wouldn't tell me. Not really. You wouldn't show me much at all. You'd smile and say something like 'maybe … maybe we all have our own paths and sometimes these paths might take us away from the ones we love but that's alright, because down the line we'll see each other again'. I don't know, I don't know if that's true anymore. I can't predict what's to come, what will happen tomorrow or when the next time I'll see you will be. Will I see you … who knows at this point? Anyways, I've been thinking, and the thing I keep going back to is … I can't have you wait for me. It's selfish of me to expect you to wait for me. I know you don't want to hear this, but I chose this path, not you. And now I'm tormented by the thought of what the world would be for us if I made the choice to stay. Hoping I get to see you all again. I love you. Yours truly, Michael.

> *He exits.*

SCENE FOURTEEN: SABOR A MÍ

Great Buckingham Street.

CHERYL *sits on the steps of her house, wrapped in her crochet blanket, waiting.* LULU *enters, coming home.*

LULU: How long have you been sitting out here?
CHERYL: Not long.
LULU: Waiting for Queenie?
CHERYL: I should have been there for you.
LULU: You two will be on good terms in no time.

> LULU *takes the seat next to* CHERYL.

You can almost see some stars tonight.
CHERYL: Not like back home.
LULU: They're still there.
CHERYL: You seem like you're in a better mood. This have anything to do with …
LULU: Johnny. I decided I didn't want to waste any more time being scared and look what happened. He told me he'll love to be my partner for the debutante.

> LULU *looks out to the street, listening to the quiet buzz of the city. She stands up from her seat.*

I'm gonna head in. The last couple of days have been a ride.
CHERYL: I'm sure this is only the beginning.
LULU: Then I better catch up on my beauty sleep. You coming in?
CHERYL: I'm gonna sit out here for a while.
LULU: Okay. Don't stay out too long.
CHERYL: Night, Lulabelle.

> LULU *heads inside.* CHERYL *takes in the quiet street, the sound of the city heard in the distance. Sirens, cars. Softly buzzing.* MILO *enters and approaches the house.*

MILO: I somehow find myself crossing those tracks once again. I'm sorry about what happened—
CHERYL: It's okay. It wasn't you who locked them up. You ever been to a mission before? When you live on the mission and under the

Aboriginal Protection Board, you don't have much of a choice in anything, really. You have a school there, where we went before we were allowed to go to school in town. A church. A hall where we have our functions. But still under the watchful eye of the mission manager who gives you rations. Depending on what mood he's in that day. If we were to go to the hospital, we'd be put in a separate wing of the building or placed outside on the verandah. There, we're given blankets and pillows with A.B.O. marked on them. Even the cutlery has the same engraving so as to not get them mixed up with the others. To make sure the white patients don't have to touch something that has come into contact with us. So, what can I do then, to become a nurse and to help? Thanks again for last night—

MILO: It was nothing.

CHERYL: Not to me. You don't have to leave. It's a nice night and if my neighbour Mr Wilson plays his piano, we might be able to catch it. You didn't have to cross those tracks for nothing—

MILO: It wasn't for nothing. Besides, I shouldn't.

CHERYL: Right.

MILO: I'm glad you're alright though, that everyone is safe. Have a good night, Sherry.

CHERYL: You too.

> MILO *leans in to kiss* CHERYL. *She pulls away.*

Milo. We—

MILO: Don't say it.

CHERYL: We can't.

MILO: We can.

CHERYL: How? How can we do any of this, when you're Ernie's friend and I'm with …

> CHERYL *stops herself.*

MILO: You won't even say it. Say it. Say his name. Say it and it'll all be over. Say it and I'll walk away right now and we never speak of it again. It'll be like it never happened.

CHERYL: We shouldn't say things we don't mean.

MILO: I mean it.

CHERYL: No, you don't.

MILO: No?

CHERYL: No, because …

MILO: What?

CHERYL: Do you know what they call guys like you?

MILO: I don't care.

CHERYL: Gin jockeys.

MILO: I don't care.

CHERYL: But you will. Trust me, you will. You'll grow tired of the stares and calls and people judging you, wondering why you picked me and not them.

MILO: So, it's about necessity then?

CHERYL: Maybe I need that. Maybe I need an easy path in my life, maybe I'll move back to the country, and live in a small house, and have children, and—

MILO: What are you afraid of, huh?

CHERYL: Everything.

MILO: And you think running away from it all is going to help?

CHERYL: I want to be in a place where I'm not being criticised by this world.

MILO: And you think it's back there? Is that what it comes down to? That you're not like me or I'm not like you, that we didn't come from the same place in this world—

CHERYL: I'm sure your mother would want you to be with a girl from your own world.

MILO: I believe my mother would want me to be with the woman I fell in love with. I'm not afraid to be seen with you, Sherry. I can't promise that you won't get the stares or the whispers while you're standing next to me. But I want you to know that I want to be with you. All of you. And if you ask me tomorrow, or the next day, or the day after that, my answer will still be the same. I want to be with you, and I have a feeling you want to be with me too.

> *Beat.*

Look, I can't compete with your past, but I can try with *now*, if you let me.

> CHERYL *thinks about it. Mr Wilson continues playing his piano, as* MILO *begins to sing 'Sherry' by The Four Seasons.*

CHERYL: Stop it. What if someone sees us?

MILO: So they see us.

> *He continues singing.*

> MILO *takes a step closer towards* CHERYL.

What do you think?

CHERYL: Of your singing?

MILO: Of me.

CHERYL: I think you have the worst timing.

MILO: I don't know about that.

> MILO *leans in and kisses* CHERYL, *as she leans into* MILO. *Music from Mr Wilson's piano becomes louder. Lights out.*

SCENE FIFTEEN: HEY LOVER

December.

Paddington Town Hall.

Debutante. Backstage. Music is playing in the main hall.

The HOST*'s voice comes through the speaker.*

HOST: Welcome ladies and gentlemen, to the 1966 debutante. Who'd have thought? A bunch of blackfullas all dressed to impress at the stunning Paddington Town Hall. Thank you everyone at the Foundation for Aboriginal Affairs for hosting this event and the hard work everyone put in to make this special night happen …

> QUEENIE *and* LULU *enter wearing their beautiful white gowns.* QUEENIE *tries to adjust her dress.*

LULU: Would you leave it alone? You're going to wrinkle it.

> LULU *tries to brush* QUEENIE*'s gown with her hand.* QUEENIE *tries to slap* LULU *away.*

Stop fidgeting.

QUEENIE: Stop, stop, stop it. Okay, I'll leave it alone. Geez, you've been so demanding.

LULU: Don't you want things to be perfect?

QUEENIE: It will be perfect if you stop fussing over me.

> QUEENIE *swats* LULU *away.*

LULU: What is with you tonight?

QUEENIE: I'm fine.

> QUEENIE *tries to peek through the curtains.*

LULU: Would you get away from that curtain?

QUEENIE: Give me a second.

LULU: Who are you looking for?

QUEENIE: No-one. I'm just looking. Is that alright with you?! I want to see who's here.

LULU: Everyone is here. The whole community. It's the event of the year. Even Bronwyn Mitchell is making an appearance.

QUEENIE: Bronwyn Mitchell?

LULU: I heard she's the special guest to close the night.

QUEENIE: You can never trust what you hear along the grapevine.

LULU: Maybe she's here to present Miss Waratah.

QUEENIE: I'll let you know once I win.

LULU: Get away from the curtains before someone sees you.

QUEENIE: No one is going to see me.

LULU: Are you nervous?

QUEENIE: What? No.

LULU: You care about this stuff.

QUEENIE: Please. Don't be stupid.

LULU: You're gonna get so many compliments.

QUEENIE: That part I do like.

LULU: See, you should have asked someone earlier instead of doing your little protest thing. Now you have no-one to dance with. Don't you feel a little stupid now?

QUEENIE: I'm not stupid, you are.

> LULU *begins looking around the space.*

What are you doing?

LULU: My glove. I must have misplaced it.

QUEENIE: Where did you last see it?

LULU: I can't go out there without it. I must have left it in the bathroom. No, wait, here it is. Wouldn't that be embarrassing? I walk out there with only one glove on. Talk about a disaster.

QUEENIE: [*sarcastically*] Yeah, the whole community would be talking about it tomorrow.

LULU: I know right?!

> LULU *slips her glove on.*

QUEENIE: Have you spoken to Sherry?

LULU: Honestly, you two avoiding each other is killing me. One of you better start talking, and soon, because I'm not here to be your messenger. I'm not running back and forth.

QUEENIE: Fine.

LULU: Fine what?

QUEENIE: Fine, I will talk to her tonight.

LULU: Thank you. This has been going on long enough.

QUEENIE: Look at you. You spent one night in lock-up and now you're ordering us around.

LULU: Things are different. From now on, I'm gonna speak up, use my voice and give you a piece of my mind, and you can take it or leave it. But to answer your question, yes, I have, I have spoken to Sherry.

QUEENIE: I haven't seen her yet.

LULU: I should check to see if Johnny is here yet.

QUEENIE: Yes, where is this partner of yours?

LULU: Johnny? He should be out there somewhere. I think he's nervous. He might be cute but he's not much of a dancer.

QUEENIE: Must be, because he missed all our dance lessons with Aunty Esther.

LULU: He couldn't get out of work.

QUEENIE: True.

LULU: Oh, this is gonna be fun, don't you think? I can't wait to get out there.

> Gliding across the dance floor.

> LULU *begins to waltz by herself. She gets carried away, bumping into* ERNIE *as he enters, wearing his tuxedo.*

Whoops.

ERNIE: Don't hurt yourself.

LULU: Sorry, Ernie. Oh, or should I say, Mr Ernest? You're looking very dapper tonight.

ERNIE: Lulabelle, looking beautiful as always. And you too, Queenie.

QUEENIE: No need, I know I look good.

ERNIE: Just take the compliment.

QUEENIE: Why do I need to take the compliment when you're just telling me something I already know?

ERNIE: Just do it.

QUEENIE: I did.

LULU: Come on, you two. Not tonight, of all nights. Can we call truce?

Feedback is heard through the speakers.

HOST: Okay. It looks like we're getting the show on the way, as we begin to present our beautiful debutantes.

LULU: Oh my goodness, it's starting! I'm gonna look for Johnny.

LULU *runs off.*

ERNIE: Is Johnny …

QUEENIE: I don't know.

QUEENIE *takes another peek out through the curtain.*

ERNIE: Looking for anyone in particular?

QUEENIE: Just looking.

ERNIE: You do look stunning, Queenie.

QUEENIE: You don't have to tell me that.

ERNIE: I know, but I also know you want to hear it.

QUEENIE: Let's get something clear. I am still doing this alone, okay, and you're—

ERNIE: Here to help.

QUEENIE: I'm winning Miss Waratah alone. Got it?

ERNIE: Got it.

QUEENIE: And can you try not to step on my feet this time?

ERNIE: How have I been stepping on your foot when you're clearly doing the wrong step?

QUEENIE: The wrong steps?!

ERNIE: Yes, do you even know what the steps are?

QUEENIE: I wouldn't have to worry about getting the steps right if you led better.

ERNIE: Hang on. If I led better?

QUEENIE: Did I stutter?

ERNIE: It would work better if you let me lead.

QUEENIE: I do let you lead but when I do, you end up doing—

ERNIE *pulls* QUEENIE *in for a kiss.* LULU *runs back into the room.*

LULU: I forgot my purse, I can't make my debut without my—oh my god!

      QUEENIE *and* ERNIE *pull away.*

Oh my god! What is going on?!

QUEENIE/ERNIE: Nothing.

LULU: Nothing?! This isn't nothing, this is more than nothing. This is … this is … What is this?!

ERNIE: It's …

LULU: I was gone for only a second, a second, and I walk into that. I mean, I knew Ernie liked you, but I never thought it would happen. I didn't think Ernie would man up enough to finally tell you.

ERNIE: Hey! I eventually got there.

QUEENIE: You knew?

LULU: Everyone knew. You two hated each other in your own special little way.

      QUEENIE *and* ERNIE *stand there quietly.* LULU *calms down.*

Sorry about all of that commotion from earlier. It's not usually like me. It was a bit shocking. I got scared for a second. Not in that way. My eyes just weren't prepared—I didn't expect that.

QUEENIE: Lulu, don't be dramatic. You're sounding like—

LULU: You, yeah, I know, it's the worst. Wait, does that mean he's your partner tonight?

QUEENIE: /No!

ERNIE: Yes.

LULU: Oh, that's wonderful. Now you don't have to do this alone.

QUEENIE: I'm still protesting.

LULU: Of course you are.

HOST: We have the lovely Cheryl-Lee Johnson and she will be accompanied by Mr Paul Ryan.

LULU: Sherry knows?

QUEENIE: Not yet.

LULU: Queenie!

QUEENIE: I know, I know, that's why I'm telling her tonight. Trust me I have it all figured out.

ERNIE: Sherry isn't going to mind. If anything, she'll be thrilled.

LULU: So this is a thing?

ERNIE *puts his arm around* QUEENIE.

This is strange for me. Don't get me wrong, I'm happy for you, the both of you. But this …

She points out their embrace.

It's different. I guess we don't get to hear your lectures anymore, Ernie. I'm gonna miss them.

ERNIE: As long as we live in the colony, there's going to be a lot of lectures on how we can break the system—

LULU: Ernie, can this wait till later? I should go find Johnny.

QUEENIE: Lulu, come on, be for real now.

LULU: For real about what?

QUEENIE: We know there isn't a Johnny.

LULU: What do you mean?

QUEENIE: He isn't coming because—

LULU: Um he is, he's just outside there.

QUEENIE: Lulu, I don't think Johnny is coming—

JOHNNY *enters, dressed in a tuxedo.*

JOHNNY: Lulu, sorry for being late. I had to close up tonight.

LULU: Johnny! It's okay. Come, come.

JOHNNY *joins* LULU.

Johnny, these are my friends, Queenie and Ernie. Everyone, this is Johnny, who is—

QUEENIE: White.

LULU: My partner for tonight.

ERNIE *elbows* QUEENIE.

QUEENIE: Right … Yes, right. Hello, Johnny. It's great to finally be meeting you.

JOHNNY: I know, it would have been sooner, but the milk bar keeps me pretty busy. She's beautiful tonight, don't you agree?

LULU: Oh stop it, you don't have to say that. I didn't tell him to say that.

QUEENIE: I believe you.

JOHNNY: Lulu, we should …

LULU: Yes, it's almost showtime.

JOHNNY: Lovely to meet you both. Lulabelle, may I?

>JOHNNY *offers his arm to* LULU *as they exit.*

HOST: And here we have Lulabelle Donovan and Lulu is accompanied by Johnny Townsend.

>ERNIE *stops and reaches in his jacket pocket. He pulls out an envelope.*

ERNIE: Before I forget. This is for you.

>*He finally gives the letter to* QUEENIE. *She opens it.*

You don't have to read it here.

QUEENIE: Then why did you give it to me now?

ERNIE: Okay, you can read it now.

>*She reads it.*

QUEENIE: You used my real name. How long have you been holding on to this?

ERNIE: You don't want to know.

>ERNIE *leans in and gives* QUEENIE *a gentle kiss.*

I'll see you out there.

>ERNIE *exits.* QUEENIE *has a moment to herself before exiting.*

HOST: Beautiful. And lucky last, we have Miss Queenie Rivers … Queenie is being accompanied by Ernest Johnson.

>*A struggle is heard as* QUEENIE *grabs the microphone.*

Wait. Hang on.

QUEENIE: I want everyone here to know that I'm doing this on my own. As protest. I want to let women know that we don't need a man to be our saviour.

>Ernest is *not* with me tonight. Okay, we're together but not together, together. He's here and I'm here. Got it!

>*The microphone is taken off* QUEENIE.

HOST: Thank you, Queenie. Okay. Ladies and gentlemen. Give a round of applause to the Foundation for Aboriginal Affairs 1966 debutantes.

>*The audience cheers.*

SCENE SIXTEEN: IN THE STILL OF THE NIGHT

Paddington Town Hall.

The crowd is loud as everyone begins mingling and dancing along to the music. CHERYL *enters the backstage area. She's wearing a long satin dress, white gloves and her pearls. She takes a moment for herself. The tag begins irritating her shoulder and she can't quite reach it. She lets out a frustrating sigh.* MILO *enters.*

> CHERYL *steps away and straightens her dress.* CHERYL *takes* MILO *in, dressed in his suit.*

MILO: You like?

CHERYL: Not too bad.

> CHERYL *tries to adjust her dress.*

MILO: Something wrong?

CHERYL: No … yes, the tag on this dress is … it's been nagging me all night … Do you mind? Gloves.

> CHERYL *turns around and* MILO *goes over her.*

MILO: Where?

CHERYL: Just there.

> MILO *rips the tag off the dress.*

MILO: When I was a kid, it was the first and last time I saw my grandparents. My nonna. Beautiful, strict lady, devoted Catholic. You'd be able to hear her rosary beads clicking and clanging in her pocket before you even laid eyes on her. One day, she was sitting in my mother's dining room, tea in hand. She didn't know much English, but she started telling me this story about her life. I don't know if she told my mother. You see, my nonna, she grew up in a well-respected family back home. When she was seventeen, she was promised to this boy. He too was from a well-off family. A banker. Uninteresting, according to Nonna. 'What am I supposed to do with numbers? I'm young, I'm beautiful, why should I marry a banker?' She had already fallen for another boy. An artist, from the next village over. She was fascinated with how he saw the world and that the world always looked beautiful through his eyes. She met him and knew that he was the man she was going to marry. So before the wedding she decided—against her parents' wishes, against the man she was promised to—that she'd run away with my nonno. And she never looked back. Have I told you how beautiful you look tonight?

CHERYL: You may have told me once or twice.

MILO: Sei bella.

CHERYL: Oh, three times?

MILO: I'll tell you every day for the rest of my life if I have to.

CHERYL: Aren't you the charmer?

MILO: It did catch your attention. My charms, my wit, my body.

> CHERYL *laughs.*

I dare you.

CHERYL: To do what?

MILO: Run away with me.

CHERYL: Anywhere?

MILO: Where you go, I go.

> CHERYL *throws her arms around* MILO *and they kiss.* LULU *enters and screams in surprise.*

LULU: Oh my god! Sorry. I'm so sorry.

> LULU *covers her eyes.*

I didn't see anything. I was just looking for you … Actually I was looking for you, Sherry. Someone said you would be back here, so I came looking for you and would you look at that, here you are … with Milo.

MILO: Hi Lulu.

CHERYL: You can take your hands away from your face.

LULU: No, no, no, it's okay. I just wanted to tell you—

> LULU *runs into some chairs.*

Ouch, son of a—I'm okay. I don't want to interrupt anything.

CHERYL: You're not.

MILO: She was.

CHERYL: Lulu, please open your eyes before you hurt yourself.

> LULU *drops her hand.*

LULU: I should really start announcing myself when I enter rooms. Um … What was I gonna say, oh yeah, Queenie is looking for you.

CHERYL: She's talking to me now?

LULU: Now, now. Enough of who's talking to who nonsense. All she said is that she has a surprise for you. Don't ask me what it is, she wouldn't tell me, but she was pretty persistent in wanting to give it to you now.

    CHERYL *thinks about it.*

I can tell her that it can wait. Maybe it'll be better for you both to talk after …

CHERYL: No, it's okay. [*To* MILO] Can you give us a moment?

MILO: Sure.

    MILO *exits.* CHERYL *stays quiet, waiting for* LULU *to respond.*

LULU: So, this is where you've been hiding.

CHERYL: I needed a break.

LULU: I can see.

    CHERYL *peeks out the curtain.*

I was speaking to a few people out there and some said it could become an annual thing. Each year, women and men get a chance to dress up and enjoy their night.

    CHERYL *takes a seat.* LULU *takes the seat next to her.*

CHERYL: You were beautiful out there tonight.

LULU: Don't start sucking up to me now.

CHERYL: No, I'm serious. Your dress, your hair, your waltz, the best one I've seen. And Johnny was a surprise there too.

LULU: He's the best. I couldn't let Queenie have all the attention.

CHERYL: Lulabelle the original go-go dancer.

LULU: I wonder what would happen once Queenie finds out. You know she hates being kept in the dark, but then again, she has this whole thing with Ernie now—

CHERYL: What thing with Ernie?

LULU: Hmm?

CHERYL: You said / there's a thing.

LULU: Did I?

CHERYL: Is there?

LULU: Umm … yes, yes, there's something going on with Ernie and Queenie. There, I said it.

CHERYL: I never thought it would ever happen.

LULU: That's what I said!

> QUEENIE *enters, wearing a sash that says, 'Miss Waratah '66' and small crown. The women cheer her on.*

QUEENIE: You like?

> QUEENIE *does a small curtsey.*

LULU: How does it feel being crowned?

QUEENIE: I told you from the very beginning I'd make a wonderful Miss Waratah and look at me now.

LULU: Helen Peterson sure was mad though. The way she looked at you when you got the crown, I was sure the ground would open up and swallow you whole.

CHERYL: You got your wish.

QUEENIE: Sometimes we deserve the little joys in life.

LULU: And you decided to ask Ernie?

QUEENIE: Hey! I couldn't ask 'man on bike' even if he looked like Mick Jagger. I mean, look at me. You think he could handle a woman like me? A woman so strong, beautiful and smart who became Miss Waratah 1966, so I—

LULU: Went and found someone that can handle you.

QUEENIE: I'm not saying that.

> *Beat.* QUEENIE *and* CHERYL *look at each other, trying to find the right words to say.*

CHERYL: I'm sorry.

QUEENIE: I don't want to fight.

CHERYL: I don't want us to fight either.

QUEENIE: I missed you.

CHERYL: I missed you too.

QUEENIE: Okay, good, because I thought I was the only one.

CHERYL: Not in your life.

QUEENIE: This is stupid. I know you didn't—

CHERYL: I would never.

QUEENIE: And you would have jumped right in after us if you could.

CHERYL: Of course.
QUEENIE: I love you, Sherry. You're my best friend.
CHERYL: You're mine.
LULU: Hey, I'm here too.
QUEENIE: Come here.

The girls cheer together, pulling into a giant hug.

Okay, enough of that! You're gonna crumple my sash.
LULU: The night was a success!
QUEENIE: It's not over yet.

QUEENIE *pulls a letter from her bust.*

LULU: Did you just pull that out of your dress?
QUEENIE: What? I have no pockets. Where else am I supposed to put it?
LULU: In your purse.
QUEENIE: I'm not carrying that thing around.
LULU: Where is it?
QUEENIE: I left it with Ernie.

QUEENIE *hands the letter over.*

A little surprise for you. It's from Michael.
CHERYL: When did you get this?
QUEENIE: Yesterday.

CHERYL *looks the letter over.*

I should get back to—
LULU: Yeah, me too.

They go to leave.

Things are really heating up with you two, huh?
QUEENIE: Shut up, Lulu, it's not like that!
LULU: Then stop blushing.
QUEENIE: I'm not blushing—it's just my make-up!
LULU: Sure it is.

SCENE SEVENTEEN: HELLO STRANGER

CHERYL *looks down at the unopened letter. She hesitates when opening it. She looks over the letter, confused—it's blank.* MICHAEL *enters back stage, wearing his uniform.*

CHERYL: Queenie, are you sure it's from—

> CHERYL *turns around to see* MICHAEL *standing in front of her.*

Michael.

MICHAEL: Hi.

> CHERYL *is frozen.*

Queenie had this brilliant idea of surprising you here. Which she wasn't wrong about. You look …

CHERYL: Why didn't you say anything to me? Why didn't you tell me you were back in the country, or the fact that I haven't heard anything from you for the past year?

MICHAEL: I'm here now.

CHERYL: Michael. I sent letters and waited and waited and nothing. For a moment there, I thought you were …

MICHAEL: I know.

CHERYL: Why didn't you …

> MICHAEL *takes a moment.*

MICHAEL: I was scared. I didn't know what was going to happen to me over there and I didn't want to make any promises I couldn't keep, especially to you. But I held on to you, till the very end.

CHERYL: Are you alright? Do you want to sit? You can sit if you want to.

MICHAEL: I'm fine. Would you like to sit?

CHERYL: Yeah, maybe.

> CHERYL *sits.* MICHAEL *sits next to her.*

MICHAEL: It's so good to see you. You don't understand how much I thought about this moment.

> *He tucks a strand of* CHERYL*'s hair behind her ear.*

You haven't changed. Now that I'm home, we can finally do all the things we wanted to do, what we've been talking about for so long. You know, start our lives together. We can go back to country, get married, kids. I don't want to waste another minute being away from you.

CHERYL *doesn't move.*

What are you doing now?

CHERYL: Now?

MICHAEL: Yeah. All I want right now is to be alone with you. We can get out of here. Go home and listen to Mr Wilson play his piano—

CHERYL: Michael—

MICHAEL: We can walk around till the sun comes up, like we used to. We can go anywhere you want.

CHERYL: What about Ernie?

MICHAEL: Ernie? What about him?

CHERYL: And Queenie and Lulu and the others out there. Everyone will be so happy to see you.

MICHAEL: Some already have, and I can see the rest another time.

MICHAEL *stops and takes a moment.*

I'm getting ahead of myself, aren't I? I'm sorry, I'm just … I'm so happy to see you … Maybe we can take things slow. You and me. You can catch me up, on everything. Take some time to get to know each other again.

CHERYL *reaches and takes* MICHAEL*'s hand.* MICHAEL *sighs.*

CHERYL: I want to stay—

MICHAEL: Okay.

CHERYL: —in Sydney. I don't want to go back to country. I'm afraid that if I go back, I'll end up staying there forever. And I don't want that. Not now. My life is here. My friends, my brother …

MICHAEL: Then we'll stay.

MICHAEL *kisses her hand.*

It'll be easy.

He kisses CHERYL *on her forehead.*

I missed you.

CHERYL: You too.

MICHAEL: I love you.

> MILO *enters,* QUEENIE *and* LULU *close behind.*

LULU: [*loud whisper*] Milo, wait.

QUEENIE: [*to* LULU] Why didn't you stop it?

LULU: Me?! If you weren't too busy kissing up on Ernie, maybe you would've had the chance to stop all this.

QUEENIE: I wasn't kissing—Hi everyone. Michael, I see you found Sherry in no time.

MICHAEL: No time at all, thanks, Queenie. You were right, she was surprised.

QUEENIE: I could imagine.

> MICHAEL *looks to* MILO.

MICHAEL: Hi mate, Michael, you are?

CHERYL: Sorry, Michael this is—

MILO: Milo.

QUEENIE: Emilio, actually.

> LULU *pinches* QUEENIE.

Ow!

MICHAEL: Milo? Oh yeah, Milo, Ernie told me about you.

MILO: Did he?

MICHAEL: Don't worry, nothing bad, Ernie would write me letters raving on and on about you and your adventures with the Freedom Rides. He spoke highly of you. He talked so much about you, I thought you were replacing me for a second.

> QUEENIE *and* LULU *laugh uncomfortably. Microphone feedback is heard through the speaker as the host approaches the stage.*

QUEENIE: Reunions are fun, aren't they …

LULU: They sure are.

QUEENIE: Maybe we should—

LULU: Yes, we should.

HOST: Check, check, check, one, two. Can you hear me? Alright. Thank you, mob, for a wonderful evening at the 1966 debutante, here at the grand Paddington Town Hall. Didn't you all look so beautiful tonight. Thank you again guests and debutantes for this magical night. And to … hang on, I lost my place, there I am, okay. And to end our magical evening, we have our very special musical guests. If you can make your way to the dance floor. Ladies and gentlemen. Miss Bronwyn Mitchell and the Black Velvets.

The band begins to play the last song of the night.

LULU: Michael, may I have this dance? I want to see if your dancing is up to scratch.

MICHAEL: I was taught by the best.

MICHAEL *goes to shake* MILO*'s hand.*

Nice to meet you, brother.

MILO: And thank you, it takes courage to do what you did.

LULU *links arms with* MICHAEL.

LULU: Come on, let's show you off to these aunties.

CHERYL: I'll be right out.

QUEENIE: Take your time.

They exit.

MILO: So that's Michael. You're right, he's very handsome.

CHERYL: You should tell him that.

MILO: He's not my type. He seems like a great guy, though.

CHERYL: He is.

MILO: Deep down, I wish he would be …

CHERYL: Horrible?

MILO: Is that bad?

CHERYL *shakes her head no.*

He's a saint.

CHERYL: I don't know about that.

MILO: I mean, I can see why you were … I can see why you're … I can see it in your face, that he means a lot to you … He brings something different out in you.

CHERYL: I know.

They stand there in silence as the music plays.

Milo—

MILO: I … I guess we have to raincheck that trip, huh?

CHERYL: You have to know … I meant everything I said to you, it's just …

MILO: Bad timing.

> CHERYL *gives a small smile.*

May I have this dance?

CHERYL: I thought you didn't dance.

> CHERYL *slips her hand into his as he pulls her in close. They begin dancing, swaying and twirling to the music as the light begins to dim.*

> *Blackout.*

THE END

BELVOIR ST THEATRE

Based in an old factory on Gadigal land, Sydney, Belvoir is one of Australia's most celebrated and beloved theatre companies. Since 1984, when a group of 600 theatre-lovers came together to buy a theatre and save it from becoming an apartment block, Belvoir has been at the forefront of Australian storytelling for the stage.

Each year the company presents an annual season of shows for this now-iconic corner stage. New work and new stories sit at the centre of Belvoir's programming, alongside a mix of reinvented classics and international writing, and a foundational commitment to Indigenous stories. In short, Belvoir is about theatrical invention, an open society, and faith in humanity.

Under the leadership of Artistic Director Eamon Flack and Executive Director Aaron Beach, Belvoir engages Australia's most prominent and promising theatre-makers. Belvoir has nurtured the talents of artists including Cate Blanchett, Simon Stone, Leah Purcell, Benedict Andrews, Tommy Murphy, Kate Mulvany, Anne-Louise Sarks, Wesley Enoch, S. Shakthidharan, and former Artistic Director Neil Armfield. Landmark productions include *Counting and Cracking*, *The Wild Duck*, *FANGIRLS*, *Cloudstreet*, *Barbara and the Camp Dogs*, *The Drover's Wife*, *Jungle and the Sea*, *Angels in America*, *Keating!*, *The Sapphires*, and many, many more. Belvoir regularly tours nationally and internationally.

Belvoir receives government support for its activities from the Federal Government through Creative Australia and the state government through Create NSW.

BELVOIR.COM.AU

BELVOIR EDUCATION

Our Education Program provides students and teachers with insights into the work of Belvoir and first-hand experiences of the theatre-making process.

PERFORMANCES

Inspiring stories, new voices, and great theatre – in the heart of Surry Hills.

Dedicated performances for schools are held throughout the year at Belvoir St Theatre

NO BARRIERS ACCESS PROGRAM

No Barriers to your students experiencing theatre.

Belvoir's No Barriers Access Program works to remove obstacles to young people experiencing and enjoying theatre.
Our programs bring students to Belvoir to see our plays and take workshops to eligible schools.

WORKSHOPS

Belvoir artists work with your students – anywhere, anytime.

Our workshops are run at Belvoir St Theatre, your school (in NSW), or online, at a time of your choosing. Students learn directly from industry artists in practical workshops, exploring performance, design, playwriting, devising, directing, technical production and more!

YOUNG BELVOIR THEATRE CLUB

Theatre makers and audiences of the future.

Our annual theatre club is for young people in Years 10, 11 and 12 who love theatre. Members attend Belvoir productions, gain insight into how productions come together and meet actors and artists.

RESOURCES

Discover how theatre is created.

Go behind the scenes into the world of Belvoir using our collection of resources online. You'll discover virtual tours, design plans and model boxes, promotion style guides, digital programs, interviews, archives and more.

FIRST CLASS

Early teaching career season ticket program.

Gain a deeper understanding of Belvoir's work and processes, connect with colleagues, develop insider industry knowledge, and get direct support and inspiration for your classroom teaching.

EDUCATION ENEWS

Sign up to stay in the loop.

Find out more about upcoming education events, schools performances, workshops and opportunities for teachers and students.

BELVOIR.COM.AU/EDUCATION/

PRODUCTION SUPPORTERS

THE
BALNAVES
FOUNDATION

ORANGES

SARDINES

Thank you to The Balnaves Foundation for generously supporting Indigenous Theatre at Belvoir St Theatre, including The Balnaves Foundation Aboriginal and Torres Strait Islander Fellowship. Dalara Williams developed *Big Girls Don't Cry* as the recipient of the 2022 Balnaves Foundation Aboriginal and Torres Strait Islander Fellowship. *Big Girls Don't Cry* was presented on the Belvoir St Theatre mainstage in the 2025 Season.

The Belvoir First Nations Creative Development Fund supports artists and productions that require the kind of time and space that sits outside our usual operating budget. By supporting First Nations Creative Development, Oranges & Sardines contributes directly to new work, innovation and risk-taking. We thank the Oranges & Sardines Foundation for investing in this incredible program.

BELVOIR SUPPORTERS

BELVOIR GIVING CIRCLES

ARTISTIC DIRECTOR'S CIRCLE

Led by Belvoir Artistic Director Eamon Flack, the Artistic Director's Circle supports an iconic Belvoir show each year; recent supported productions include *Into the Woods* in 2023, *August: Osage County* in 2024 and *King Lear* in 2025. Being a member of the Artistic Director's Circle is a rewarding opportunity to take an active role in Belvoir's development and contribute to our most ambitious work.

Patty Akopiantz &
Justin Punch
Sophie &
Stephen Allen
The Balnaves Foundation
Guido Belgiorno-Nettis AM &
Michelle Belgiorno-Nettis
Anne Britton
Jillian Broadbent AC FRSN
Andrew Cameron AM &
Cathy Cameron
Sue Donnelly
David Gonski AC &
Assoc. Prof. Orli Wargon OAM
Fee &
David Hancock
Alison Kitchen
Ian Learmonth &
Julia Pincus
Helen Lynch AM &
Helen Bauer
Sam Meers AO
Karen Moses
Mountain Air Foundation
Beau Neilson
Kerr Neilson
Paris Neilson
Stuart &
Kate O'Brien
Cathie &
Paul Oppenheim

Dan &
Jackie Phillips
Andrew Price
Sherry-Hogan Foundation
Rob Thomas AO
The WeirAnderson Foundation
Kim Williams AM &
Catherine Dovey
Rosie Williams &
John Grill AO
Cathy Yuncken

THE GROUP

Led by Belvoir Board member Louise Thurgood Phillips, The Group is a collective of inspiring likeminded women committed to supporting female creatives and bringing more women's stories to the Belvoir stage. In 2025, The Group is supporting *Orlando* – previous productions include *Never Closer, The Weekend, Tell Me I'm Here, Stop Girl, A Room of One's Own*, and *FANGIRLS*.

Patty Akopiantz
Sophie Allen
Jessica Block
Margaret Butler
Louise Campbell
Johanna Featherstone
Jennie Gao
Jane-Maree Hurley
Kirsty Kovacs
Robin Low
Sandra McCullagh
Sam Meers AO
Karen Moses
Julie-Anne Lacko
Naomi O'Brien
Elizabeth Pakchung
Rebel Penfold-Russell OAM
The Phillips Family
Sabrina Quick
Sue Rosen
Victoria Taylor

THE HIVE

THE HIVE is a community of professionals and creatives, connected through a love of theatre. Donations to THE HIVE support a new work at Belvoir each year, starting with *The Wrong Gods* in 2025, to help pave the way for the next generation of theatre-makers in Sydney and beyond.

HIVE AMBASSADORS

Dan Chesterman
Johanna Featherstone
Piers Grove
Alicia Gunn
Zach Kitschke
Tommy Murphy
Teya Phillips
Matt Rossi

HIVE CHAMPIONS

Dan Chesterman
Matt Rossi
Zach Kitschke

HIVE MEMBERS

Brian Abel
Mollie Anderson
Alex Badran
Aaron Beach
Justin Butterworth
Catherine D.
James M Garvey
Alicia Gunn
Samantha Jones
Clancy King
Nicolas Mason
Nathan Moses
Julia Newbould
Salleigh Olsen
Leigh Sanderson
Steph Sands
Martyn Thompson

BELVOIR DONORS

Thank you to the visionary donors who have committed to a level of financial support that allows us to realise our creative ambitions and share passionate, diverse and surprising contemporary Australian theatre with audiences here, across the country and across the globe.

$50,000 AND ABOVE

The Balnaves Foundation
Blake Beckett Trust
Andrew Cameron AM &
Cathy Cameron
Doc Ross Family Foundation
John &
Libby Fairfax
Ian Learmonth &
Julia Pincus
Playking Foundation
The Neilson Foundation
The Nelson Meers Foundation

$20,000-$49,999

Patty Akopiantz &
Justin Punch
Copyright Agency
Cultural Fund
Girgensohn Foundation
Fee &
David Hancock
Marion Heathcote &
Brian Burfitt
Libby Higgin &
Dr Gae Anderson
Victoria Holthouse
Houston Group
Ingrid Kaiser
The Kerridge Foundation
James N Kirby Foundation
The Knights Family Jabula
Foundation
Anne &
Mark Lazberger

Ross Littlewood &
Alexandra Curtin
Helen Lynch AM &
Helen Bauer
Millari Family Trust
Karen Moses
Mountain Air Foundation
Cathie &
Paul Oppenheim
Oranges &
Sardines
Dan &
Jackie Phillips
Kim Williams AM &
Catherine Dovey

$10,000-$19,999

Sophie &
Stephen Allen
Guido Belgiorno-Nettis AM &
Michelle Belgiorno-Nettis
Anne Britton
Jillian Broadbent AC FRSN
Constructability Recruitment
Bob &
Chris Ernst
Louise Flanagan
Gandevia Foundation
Anita Jacoby AM
Johnson Family Foundation
The Keir Foundation
Alison Kitchen
Matana Foundation
Cynthia Nadai &
Roslyn Burge
Panthera
Rachel Emma
Ferguson Foundation
Rebel Penfold-Russell OAM
David Pumphrey OAM &
Jill Pumphrey
The Roberts Pike Foundation
The Roger Allen and Maggie
Gray Foundation
Penelope Seidler AM
Sherry-Hogan Foundation
Victoria Taylor
Rob Thomas AO

Judy Thomson
The Wales Family Foundation
The WeirAnderson Foundatic
Shemara Wikramanayake &
Ed Gilmartin
Rosie Williams &
John Grill AO
Cathy Yuncken

$5,000-$9,999

Arun Abey
Colin &
Richard Adams
Claire Armstrong &
John Sharpe
Jessica Block
Jan Burnswoods
Dan &
Emma Chesterman
Chrysanthemum Foundation
Bernard Coles KC &
Margaret Coles
Hartley &
Sharon Cook
Sue Donnelly
Mark &
Jane Fulton
Jennie Gao
Danny &
Kathleen Gilbert
The Greatorex Fund
Bill Hawker &
Mary Bolt
Houston Group
Jane-Maree Hurley
Zach Kitschke
Bruce Meagher &
Greg Waters
Peter &
Jan Shuttleworth
Jann Skinner
Chris &
Bea Sochan
Annie Williams
Toni Wren

SPECIAL THANKS

We thank our Life Members, who have made outstanding contributions to Belvoir over more than thirty years. They have changed the course of the company and are now ingrained in its fabric.

Neil Armfield AO, Neil Balnaves AO, Andrew Cameron AM, David Gonski AC, Rachel Healy, Louise Herron AM, Sue Hill, Geoffrey Rush AC, Orli Wargon OAM, and Chris Westwood.

We would also like to acknowledge our Legacy Donors, for making a dramatic difference by remembering Belvoir in their Wills: Len Armfield, Liz Barton, Brian Carey, Sharan Daly, Nick Enright, Ronald Falk, Diane Hague, Samantha Jones, Jann Kohlman, Patricia McEnerny, Cajetan Mula, Geoffrey Scharer, Ronald Thompson, and Shirley June Warland. We will always remember their generosity.

Thank you to the generous individuals and Foundations supported the redevelopment of Belvoir Street Theatre and the purchase of our Warehouse in 2005 & 2006, and the renovation of our theatre foyer and bathrooms in 2024.

Andrew & Cathy Cameron
(Refurbishment of theatre and warehouse)

Russell Crowe
(Redevelopment of theatre)

The Gonski Foundation & The Nelson Meers Foundation
(Gonski Meers Foyer)

Andrew & Wendy Hamlin
(Executive Director's office)

Hal Herron
(The Hal Bar)

The Nelson Meers Foundation
(Sam's Bar)

Geoffrey Rush
(Redevelopment of theatre)

Fred Street AM
(Upstairs dressing room)

BELVOIR PARTNERS

If your business would like to partner
with Belvoir, please email us at
development@belvoir.com.au
or call **02 8396 6250**

www.ingramcontent.com/pod-product-compliance
Lightning Source LLC
Chambersburg PA
CBHW050017090426
42734CB00021B/3303